Freire and Student Empowerment

Freire and Student Empowerment

Voice, Agency, and Transformative Pedagogies

EDITED BY
MICHAELA L. ENSWEILER

BLOOMSBURY ACADEMIC
LONDON · NEW YORK · OXFORD · NEW DELHI · SYDNEY

BLOOMSBURY ACADEMIC
Bloomsbury Publishing Plc, 50 Bedford Square, London, WC1B 3DP, UK
Bloomsbury Publishing Inc, 1359 Broadway, New York, NY 10018, USA
Bloomsbury Publishing Ireland, 29 Earlsfort Terrace, Dublin 2, D02 AY28, Ireland

BLOOMSBURY, BLOOMSBURY ACADEMIC and the
Diana logo are trademarks of Bloomsbury Publishing Plc

First published in Great Britain 2026

Series design by Charlotte James
Cover image © Paulo Freire via Torres, Carlos Alberto (2014).
First Freire: Early writings in social justice education. Teachers College Press.
Background image © ilyast / Getty Images

ISBN: HB: 978-1-3504-6392-9
          PB: 978-1-3504-6393-6
        ePDF: 978-1-3504-6396-7
       eBook: 978-1-3504-6395-0

Series: Freire in Focus

Typeset by Integra Software Services Pvt. Ltd.
Printed and bound in in Great Britain

For product safety related questions contact productsafety@bloomsbury.com.

To find out more about our authors and books visit www.bloomsbury.com
and sign up for our newsletters.

CONTENTS

FIGURES

CONTRIBUTORS

Fadhila Hadjeris is a PhD candidate in Social Sciences and Comparative International Education in the School of Education at the University of California, Los Angeles, USA. Fadhila's research interests focus on foreign language education in Algeria, the politics of language and identity, and the influence of globalization and neoliberal reforms on the experiences of teachers and learners in the Global South. Her most recent article is "Colorism and Indigeneity: The Portrayal of Tuareg Amazighs in EFL Textbooks in Algeria" (2024).

Brian Zamora is a doctoral student at the University of California, Los Angeles in the School of Education and Information Studies. His research interests focus on using sociocultural theories of learning and critical qualitative methodologies alongside theories of place to understand urban formations of learning in everyday life.

Darek M. Ciszek is a PhD student in Education at the University of California, Los Angeles. His research interests focus on LGBTQ-inclusive curriculum, educational psychology, and social development. He has presented his research at the American Educational Research Association (AERA), the British Psychological Society (BPS), and the Comparative and International Educational Society (CIES).

Monte Joffee is Chair of the Board of Trustees of The Renaissance Charter School and The Renaissance Charter School Two in New York City. His research interests include charter schools, Global Citizenship Education, the evolving field of "Soka education," school culture, and new school formation. His most recent publication is a chapter in Bosio & Guajardo (eds), *Value-Creating Education: Teachers' Perceptions and Practice* (2024).

Sara A. Tirschwell is a turnaround executive and is currently the Interim Chief Business Transformation Officer of The Hain Celestial Group, Inc. She spent over thirty years on Wall Street as one of the few leading women in the field of distressed finance and restructuring. As a Republican candidate for New York City Mayor in 2020–21, she repeatedly advocated for P-12 educational reform and investment in early childhood education.

T. Willard Fair was President and CEO of the Urban League of Greater Miami, where he served from 1963 to 2025. He has received over 200 service awards. Together with then Governor Jeb Bush, Fair co-founded the first charter school in Florida. Fair volunteered in a local elementary school classroom where he was a role model, hands-on innovator, and supporter for the classroom teacher. He co-directs "The Will to Achieve" (www.willtoachieve.org), an initiative to bring disruptive innovation to American P-12 education. Most recently, he was interviewed on "Face to Face with Jonathan Small" (https://www.youtube.com/live/frKC0cX_2wg).

Tai Abrams is the founder and CEO of AdmissionSquad, a 501(c)(3) helping high-achieving middle schoolers gain admission into top NYC high schools. Her student experience at one such school propelled her to Mathematics degrees from Duke University and Brooklyn College. She envisions students of color in NYC being able to follow her path and gain increased access to opportunity. AdmissionSquad has worked with over 1200 students and has maintained an 80 percent success rate in getting clients into a top NYC high school.

Michaela L. Ensweiler M.S.Ed is a PhD candidate in Social Sciences and Comparative Education at the University of

California, Los Angeles. Her research focuses on ecopedagogy through a food lens hoping to enact change in the space of food pedagogy. She has published articles and presented at various conferences including but not limited to AERA, CIES, NAAEE, and NCTE concerning unsustainable, dominant forms of food and education systems. Her most recent article concerns agroecological ethos in a postdigital world which can be found in the Encyclopedia of Postdigital Science and Education (2023). She is the founder and CEO of Duck on the Fox LLC to consult in areas of ecopedagogical pedagogies.

Moraima Machado Ed.D. is an elementary school principal in the San Lorenzo Unified School District with eight years of leadership experience. She also serves as a leadership coach at the Principal Leadership Institute (PLI) at UC Berkeley. Her research interests center on collaborating with teachers, parents, and community members to utilize critical pedagogy and storytelling as the foundation for reimagining and creating engaging, socially just learning environments for marginalized students. She received her doctorate in Educational Leadership at East Carolina University in 2021. Her dissertation is entitled Family Stories Matter: Critical Pedagogy of Storytelling in Fifth-grade Classrooms.

Maria Guajardo is Professor of Leadership Studies in the Faculty of International Liberal Arts at Soka University, Japan. Her research is at the intersection of global leadership, global citizenship education, women, and critical pedagogy. She is an author, international trainer, and motivational speaker. Her most recent book is *Value-Creating Education: Teachers' Perceptions and Practice* (2024).

Cae Rodrigues is Professor at the Federal University of Sergipe in the Department of Physical Education. His research interests focus on ecophenomenology, ecopedagogies, and environmental justice linked to the access to nature. He has been an honorary visiting researcher at La Trobe University and at the University of the Sunshine Coast (Australia), at the University of Lille (France), and at the University of Bologna (Italy). He is the current Editor of Special Editions for *The Journal of Environmental Education*, and has published on environmental education and ecopedagogy, environmental justice, socioenvironmental conflicts at the coast, and environmental leisure theory.

Brent Blair is Professor of Practice at the USC School of Dramatic Arts where he is founder of the Institute for Theatre & Social Change (ITSC). He trained in voice with Kristin Linklater and Theatre of the Oppressed with Augusto Boal. His research is currently focused on interactive theater with communities fighting antidemocratic cultures, particularly looking at the intersection of healing and justice in Los Angeles, India, Rwanda, and Israel-Palestine. He has written on Theatre of the Oppressed in situations of collective trauma, with youth, and in restorative justice settings.

Introduction

In May of 2022, the University of California—Los Angeles, Soka University, and the University of Southern California collaborated to build a global convention of Freirean scholars to celebrate the Centennial birthday of Paulo Freire. The conference, titled "Education, Democracy, and Citizenship: A Celebration of Paul Freire's Centennial," brought together over sixty presenting participants and many contributions behind the scenes. Global perspectives regarding pedagogy, politics, sustainability, and citizenship were reported from various locales such as Spain, Lithuania, Portugal, Malta, Argentina, China, South Korea, South Africa, Brazil, Norway, and the United States. Thoughtful questions and conversations brewed critical thought and careful considerations. Book launches were introduced, and five outstanding keynote speakers led participants in pondering the future of Freirean thought for years to come. From this remarkable event, this book brings a handful of these future ponderings to you, the reader, in consideration of how Freire empowers our students.

I'd like to acknowledge Darek Ciszek, MPA and PhD student at UCLA in co-creating this book's prospectus and co-writing this introduction. He has been an integral part of the creation of this publication and an exceptional colleague in my educational journey.

From the many readings of Paulo Freire, it is apparent that education is a tool for liberation. Through critical thought, reflections, transformations, dialog, and praxis, education is a unified vision of hope for its students. This publication is timely— in this crucial time of political, educational, and ecological unrest, this book offers these themes at a birds-eye glance with practical experiences inside and outside formal learning spaces. Critical theories, vis-à-vis education and pedagogical design, are needed to help stem the tide of growing educational, economic, and political inequalities. Inside these chapters, many examples of these inequalities can be found—stemming from the rise of policies aimed at censoring and silencing educational content as well as educator and student voices, social and planetary inequities and harm, standardization of a neoliberal curriculum and competitive meritocracy, and educator and student disempowerment and fragmentation. This work seeks to focus the lens on students' experiences in and outside of formal classrooms and what educators can do, in Freirean fashion, to empower them as critical global citizens from the views of several authors who have researched alternative and critical ways of learning and knowing through a variety of Freirean-based approaches.

Within academia, there is an important need to learn how to apply these Freirean concepts in spaces of learning and, in turn, help educators create and promote spaces that nurture said themes as well as student agency, autonomy, and self-efficacy. This book, which is part of a larger series of practical Freirean tenets, focuses on the myriads of ways in which educators and learners can be co-intentional in their approach to student learning and foster pedagogies that raise potential for conscientization, dialog, and transformational praxis. In doing so, this book highlights curriculum adaptations, social and planetary justice models, educator support, and student empowerment for educators of all kinds to reflect on as they explore new venues of empowering their learners and surrounding communities (and vice-versa) in a way that is critically Freirean research-based and broadened through the author's wide-ranging diversity.

This publication is divided into two parts: the first part focuses on Freirean theory that appears in classrooms and is the basis for the practical chapters in the second part. The second part explores transformative education models as well as curricula and pedagogy that serve to disrupt the standardized "banking model" Freire spoke of in *Pedagogy of the Oppressed* (1970) of current formal education models. This part serves to elaborate from theory to the classrooms and communities students inhabit and seeks to empower readers to solve inequities and invest in their future as critically awoken Freirean agents of hope and change.

Chapters Overview

Each chapter utilizes a unique Freirean tenet operated to disrupt traditionally silencing forms of education. Within the following pages, authors highlight their own experiences, reflections, and praxis in educational spaces to highlight how Freire has inspired them to not only challenge these upsetting trends, but also empower their students toward greater hope and liberation.

In the first chapter, our author highlights educational issues that prevent the achievement of democratic citizenship. Through reflections on Bourdieu and Freire, we see a central question emerging about how to invest in educational spaces to cultivate critically conscious individuals who are prepared to see through the challenges presented in today's globalized world and into unforeseen challenges that may arise in our always advancing future. We see this grow from a local context to global citizenship, a tenet of Freire, suggesting ways to empower learners to promote equitability and inclusive pedagogical practices for cohesive learning environments.

In the second chapter, our author speaks to place-based learning models that aid learners in reclaiming their local and indigenous histories and identities within Chicanx communities. Starting from looking at the concrete—who and where learners and educational spaces are and how identity is formed from this space is the beginning of critical consciousness, another tenet of Freire. With these local places and identities in mind, learners can become empowered to then reach out globally, as locally informed citizens, to be critically conscious global citizens. Through the eyes of a case study, learners speak about how analyzing place aids in (re) connecting them to their identity and becoming empowered through place-based inquiry. Through this recognition of their identity, they can become critically aware of other identities and utilize this knowledge to collaborate on the global scale for transformational praxis.

The third chapter reviews how queer/education advocates can utilize Freire to frame critical conversations that surround the outlawing and further silencing of LGBTQ+ voices in traditional P-12 educational spaces. Our author utilizes Freire's dialogical forms of learning, dialog being a tenet, to place these critical conversations surrounding the silencing and oppression of LGBTQ+ learners. Through these dialogical practices, learners can become aware of their and many of their colleagues' oppression—reaching conscientization and becoming pillared agents of hopeful and transformational praxis.

Our fourth and final chapter in the first part of this publication writes a letter to learners informing them of two ideas put forth by Freire—"limit situations" and the "culture of silence." With these troubling concepts in mind, the letter delves into preparing learners to change the traditional American P-12 schools themselves. Utilizing their diverse voices in unified dialog, a tenet of Freire, this chapter expounds a plethora of ideas and practices learners can operationalize activism to become empowered agents of hope and change within their community, and collectively, creating a ripple of impact. The chapter specifically instructs and informs learners what to expect and how to perform three steps of activism to achieve this.

Our first chapter in the second part is self-written as a contribution of ecopedagogy in elementary learning spaces.

This part begins with younger learners and progresses to spaces of tertiary education. The chapter is set as a lesson plan educators can potentially enact to further learners in examining sociopolitical and ecological acts of violence to transform these systems of oppression into more sustainable and loving systems of care for human and nonhuman entities.

The sixth chapter considers storytelling in educational spaces as a form of critical literacy and antiracist education for youth. Our author challenges the traditional Eurocentric models of American curricula and schooling in aiding diverse voices of color to share their experiences in these spaces thus centering their place and identities in an act of inclusivity. Learners were able to examine their identity through family, reflection, and dialog, which are tenets of Freire, to enrich the classroom chorus. With this dialog, the classroom dynamics changed substantially, which our author describes in this chapter.

The seventh chapter of this publication moves us from elementary grades and focuses on student-centered learning approaches in higher education that empowers women leadership. Through practices of critical pedagogy and global citizenship education, two tenets of Freire, we can challenge traditional forms of educational practices that tend to silence and place hierarchy upon diverse gender expression. Through the process of trial and error, and of "reading the world," and challenging power dynamics in traditional systems and structures, our author utilizes critical and globally informed teaching strategies that awakened learners to their power and determination to embody greater roles in becoming agents of hope and change—globally informed and empowered leaders.

In the eighth chapter, ecopedagogy is introduced in higher education settings as opposed to an elementary school setting earlier in this part. Through ecological readings of the world, our author explores reflections and praxis as embodied action with human and nonhuman entities. Through educational spaces that promote learning through caring and love, instead of the traditionally violent act of banking education, learners are able to reproduce love and care instead of violence. This love and care reverberate in all that our learners do—creating hopeful and loving agents of change for human and nonhuman entities. This is something Freire strived for; through these tenets, he wanted to be remembered as someone who loved all entities.

The ninth and final chapter in the publication progresses to higher education and centers us in the "Theater of the Oppressed"—an act of restorative justice that utilizes learners as players in the theatrical "performances" of oppression. This act can be seen as a tenet of Freire as well—learners have read these acts of oppression in their world, however, through (re)performing them, they are then able to rewrite them—an act of conscious and critical transformational praxis. Our author examines the past five years of USC's collaboration with Healing Dialogue and Action to read and rewrite the oppressive narratives of the American carceral system.

Within these chapters you will hear from the diverse voices of our authors and explore tenets of Paulo Freire that can be implemented in a variety of educational spaces. We hope this publication will inspire you to examine educational practices and utilize these Freirean tenets to empower your learners in becoming agents of hope, transformation, and love for all entities, just like Paulo Freire.

CHAPTER ONE

Reading Freire and Bourdieu in Local Educational Systems: Implications for Teachers' and Students' Empowerment

Fadhila Hadjeris

Introduction

Following the 2030 agenda on Sustainable Development Goals drafted by the UN in 2015, reframing educational systems within national contexts became a priority for individual nation-states. The central question that emerges in this context is how to invest in our educational institutions to cultivate well-informed individuals prepared for the challenges of today's globalized world? I embarked on this chapter not to answer this question directly but to highlight educational issues that are likely to hinder the realization of democratic citizenship, particularly in postcolonial contexts. I will address this theme by drawing on the philosophical contributions of Freire and Bourdieu. The framework that each has proposed serves as a useful tool that could be used as a lens to propose a bottom-up philosophy that is compatible with local context. The aim of the chapter is twofold. First, I will provide a brief analysis of the centralized education system and its potential drawbacks. Second, I will employ Freire's (1970, 2005) concepts to highlight their relevance in empowering teachers and learners as well as fostering more inclusive, equitable, and humanistic pedagogical practices. I will then draw on Bourdieu's insights to demonstrate how Freire's transformative praxis can be reimagined and reinvented to critically address the ways education simultaneously acts as a site of social and cultural reproduction.

Challenges of National Public Education: Personal Reflections

Neoliberalism is a political economic theory, which juxtaposes the advancement of "human well-being" with the promotion of "entrepreneurial skills" (Harvey, 2005). Neoliberalism theory is guided by three principles: privatization, competition, and the minimum intervention of the nation-state (Harvey, 2005; Piller & Cho, 2013; Torres, 2017). Living in a globalized world that is driven by neoliberal ideologies, we are witnessing and experiencing a proliferation of numerous issues and crises affecting our planet. These include, but are not limited to wars, racism, social injustice, growing inequality, discourses of intolerance and hate, climate change, and global pandemics, among others. The growing of these challenges calls for the need for a new form of education that would make sense both at the local and the global levels.

The framework of Global Citizenship Education (GCE) was first suggested in Global Education First Initiative meeting when the then-UN Secretary-General, Ban Ki-moon, put the goal of fostering global citizenship on the top of its agenda among the two other goals of putting every child in school and improving the quality of learning (GEFI, 2012). It was then revisited in the 2030 agenda on Sustainable Development Goals by the UN in the 2015 meeting where fostering global citizenship is highlighted under goal 4.7.[1] As a new educational model and a plan of action, GCE underscores the integration of knowledge, skills, and ethical values that enable learners to critically think and engage with issues of global concern (Andreotti, 2010; Torres, 2017; UNESCO, 2014; 2015; 2018). The key objective of this model is to add value to national citizenship education (Torres, 2017). Educating for global citizenship is based on three "global commons": acknowledging the planet as our home with a commitment to protect its resources, global peace, and lastly advocating for democratic citizenship with equal rights and dignified life to all individuals regardless of their differences (Torres & Bosio, 2020). Despite its aspirational goals, GCE remains a broad, complex, and contested concept (Shultz, 2007; Jorgenson & Shultz, 2012; Tawil, 2013). Consequently, it has become one of the most significant areas of educational research (Abdi et al., 2015; Sant et al., 2018).

The achievement of GCE goals at the national level is to some extent challenging, specifically in contexts where education is utilized as a tool that reproduces privilege and oppression (Green, 1990). In other words, what would hinder the achievement of global peace, sustainability, and justice is that our national education systems are built around ideologies that perpetuate division more than unity, superiority of the self vs. inferiority of the other more than acknowledgment of our belonging to common humanity, and prejudice and intolerance rather than dialog. Apple (1993) employed the concept of "politics of accords or compromises" to highlight how these ideologies are instilled through consent, creating the social conditions to achieve these compromises. These social conditions include standardized curriculum, standardized tests, and unquestioned pedagogy; all contribute to the reproduction of the status quo and prevent the cultivation of citizens who have the spirit of critical thinking. In highlighting the difference in schooling between democratic and undemocratic societies, Apple (1991) writes:

> For some groups of people, schooling is seen as a vast engine of democracy-opening horizons, ensuring mobility, and so on. For others, the reality of schooling is strikingly different. It is seen as a form of social control or, perhaps, as the embodiment of cultural dangers, institutions whose curricula and teaching practices threaten the moral universe of the students who attend them.
>
> (p. 1)

Starting with the school curriculum, standardized textbooks are used to instill in learners' specific knowledge, values, and skills that influence learners' formation of their characters, attitudes, and personal development (Al-Nawashi, 2012). A cross-countries analysis of school textbooks reveals that the content is centered on the legitimization of one's local culture and the marginalization or stereotypical depiction of the others' culture (Al-Nawashi, 2012; Wiseman, 2014; Bishara, 2020; Hadjeris, 2024).

Apart from the textbook content, the culture standardized testing and the mechanisms of private tutoring, which became a global phenomenon, reveal the limitations of our education systems that are built on neoliberal ideologies. In other words, they focus more on teaching for exam preparation and less on the ethics and the humanistic values that are needed in today's globalized society. With the treatment of education as a commodity, its role shifted to "mechanical" rather than "educative" teaching. More specifically, the importation of these reforms in postcolonial context shifted the focus of education from that of instilling good values that contribute to learners' growth and creativity to a form of education that fosters the spirit of competition leading to more disparities among the disadvantaged and advantaged students.

In addition to the state's control of education throughout the curriculum and standardized testing ideology, another problematic factor is "the banking system of education" (Freire, 1970), which is attributed to three reasons. First, the prescribed school curriculum does not give teachers enough flexibility to teach perspectives beyond the dominant culture. Second, teachers' pedagogy in their class reflects the way they have been trained, which leads to the vicious cycle of reproducing certain ideologies and ways of being. The third reason, which is even more intricate, is the adoption of successive Western-imported school reforms[2] that are not strategically scrutinized. These factors together with the lack of material resources and the insufficient professional development of teachers put most of them in situations of incapability to interrogate what is being prescribed. The interplay of all these factors does not only perpetuate ideologies that reproduce unequal social structures but also facilitate the process of engaging in mechanical way of teaching/learning which disempowers both teachers and learners.

Possibilities for Social Transformation: A Freirean Perspective

Broadly speaking, education can play a dual role: "a means for social control and/or a force for liberation" (Green, 1990). Freire (1970), the pioneer of critical pedagogy, introduced the concept of "banking education" to emphasize the role of schools in maintaining structures of oppression. Within this framework, individuals are treated as passive recipients to be filled with "communiqué" that is detached from their existential reality (p. 72). To move beyond this "one-sided" framework that fosters mechanical instruction and sustains the status quo, Freire advocated for "a problem-posing" form of education that is based on the problematization rather than the uncritical acquisition of facts. Teachers' and learners' empowerment[3] is at the heart of Freire's critical pedagogy. Freire (1970, 2005) endorsed the concept of "conscientizaçao" (critical consciousness), which urges the individual to develop awareness of the social, political, and economic conditions that oppress them as well as the capacity to act toward their transformation. For Freire, human beings are endowed with mental abilities to control their own destiny. According to Freire (2005), "men are not *in* the world but *with* the world" (p. 3, emphasis in original). As such, to empower their learners, educators are required to develop a spirit of critical thinking rather than passively adjust as objects incapable of changing their reality and easily manipulated by top-down myths. This critical mindfulness elevates man's status from a state of "naïve transitivity" associated with irrational and illogical mythical reality to a "critical transitive consciousness" that is inclusive, rational, and scientific (Freire, 2005).

To cultivate this pedagogy of empowerment, educators' practice should not be devoid of "praxis"; a pedagogical act that involves a constant process of both reflection and action (Freire, 1970). Reflection implies literacy; hence one's ability to successfully read the word; however, unless this literacy is linked with the existential reality of the learners, it would be useless as it would rather alienate the individual.

Freire (1970) set up the foundations for teachers and learners to engage in the process of depoliticizing education through transforming the imbalance of power existing between the oppressed and the oppressor. This form of transformation brings about social change that secures humanity and dignity to all individuals regardless of their cultural, socioeconomic, gender, or educational background. Critical consciousness is not enough for the humanization of education. Freire also emphasized the aspect of the collective, which makes his pedagogy pertinent. This aspect thrives when both teachers and learners engage in dialog, learn from each other, and empower each other for the purpose of liberation from all sorts of inequality and injustices. Freire (1970) clarifies:

Through dialogue, the teacher-of-the students and the students-of-the teacher cease to exist and a new term emerges: teacher-student with students-teachers. The teacher is no longer purely the-one-who-teaches, but one who is himself taught in dialogue with the students, who in turn while being taught also teach. They become jointly responsible for a process in which all grow ... in order to function, authority must be *on the side* of freedom, not *against* it.

(p. 80, emphasis in original)

Therefore, through depoliticizing education and engaging educators and learners in this process of transformation of the status quo, Freire's pedagogy could be considered as an effective tool to liberate educational sites from all sorts of hegemony. As such, the empowered individual would invest in one's experiences and critical consciousness to combat the different stereotypes and oppressive ideologies and ultimately advocate for a dignified life for all human beings as well as for the protection of the mother Earth.

Education for Social/Cultural Reproduction: Bourdieu's Perspective

Freire's work has been and continues to inform the work of different scholars as well as to be reinvented in different contexts. For instance, there are many intersections between the concepts developed by Freire and the work of the sociologist Pierre Bourdieu. Using a critical lens, Bourdieu (1989) has emphasized the process of social transformation through challenging the power of "world-making" (p. 23). In Bourdieu & Passeron (1970), there is a juxtaposition of the term "symbolic violence" with any act that uses force to impose meanings as legitimate and involves concealing the power relations. They highlighted three factors that sustain the status quo. First, the recruitment of specific agents, such as education inspectors to maintain the dominant culture and the exclusion of anyone who may pose the risk of integrating any work that does not align with this culture. Second, establishing standardized and controlled training and instruments. Third, standardizing the school culture as the "routinized culture." Despite the key role that teachers play as the agents of change, these factors facilitate their unconscious assimilation into the system through what Bourdieu and Passeron (1970) referred to as "la fonctionnarisation" (bureaucratization), whereby teachers are not only incognizant of this objective reality, but also in a state of "désintéressement" (selflessness) neglecting their own interest to serve the interest of the power.

In terms of the transmission of the material at the school level, Bourdieu and Passeron (1970) used the concept of "pedagogic authority" which grants teachers power and entitles them to assume the legitimate right of imposition, e.g., the use of tools of punishment that are socially acceptable. The outcome of this blend of "banking education" (Freire, 1970) model is the uncritical internalization of the material by the learners. Two perils follow from this pedagogic act of imposition. First, the learner's failure to recognize the objective reality of the imposed arbitrary culture as irrational since both the content and the power relations are taken for granted. Instead, the mechanical way of learning prevents the development of the learners' critical consciousness and the use of their mental faculties to make sense of the surrounding environment. Second, instructing the learners to accept and internalize the dominant culture as the only legitimate culture runs the risk of cultivating individuals who are not open and tolerant to other cultures. The output of the delivery and internalization of the cultural arbitrary through the pedagogic action contributes to the formation of the individual's character, i.e., "habitus": "a system of schemes of perception and appreciation of practices, cognitive, and evaluative structures which are acquired through the lasting experience of a social position ...

it implies a 'sense of one's place' but also a 'sense of the place of others'" (Bourdieu, 1989, p. 19). Characterized as "formation durable," habitus lasts even after the end of the pedagogic action (Bourdieu & Passeron, 1970). According to Bourdieu, the interaction of the "pedagogic work" through teachers enacting standardized curriculum, "pedagogic action" through the transmission of material, and "pedagogic authority" through the teacher–learner asymmetrical relationship leads to the generation of "Doxa." It is defined as: "the way the natural and the social world is typically constructed as *self-evident*. The condition of doxa sets the limits of the thinkable and the sayable-the possible universe of discourse" (cited in Levinson, 2011, p. 123, my emphasis). This process of indoctrination serves three functions: (1) it assigns everyone an identity, (2) it dictates to people their duties given who they are through speech acts (e.g., directives), and (3) it announces what people have done. In each case, it "imposes a point of view, that of the institution … This point of view is instituted as *legitimate*, that is, a point of view that *everyone* has to recognize at least within the boundaries of *a definite society*" (Bourdieu, 1989, my emphasis). Thus, this one-sided direction of discourse denies the subordinate group the right of participation or decision about their own destiny as the ruling class is entitled to assume the power of "world-making" (Bourdieu, 1989), and thereby the construction of "the national identity" (Bourdieu, Wacquant & Farage, 1994).

Bourdieu (1989) unveiled the conditions that lead to the state of human disempowerment, namely, the dehumanization of a category of people by the privileged and powerful elite leading to unjust social situations. To interrupt the status quo, he advocates for a transformation that is initiated by and involves the powerless. One prerequisite for the achievement of this goal is the development of awareness about the conditions that maintain their subjugation.

Conclusion

This chapter is driven by my reflections as both an educator within a centralized system of education and a lifelong learner. It seeks to diagnose the social conditions that generate and perpetuate systems of privilege and oppression while simultaneously exploring alternative pathways for social transformation. Central to this transformation is the empowerment of teachers and learners, which necessitates a critical conversation between the theories of Freire and Bourdieu.

Freire offers robust tools to cultivate autonomous, critical, and enlightened individuals who continuously educate themselves to achieve democratic citizenry. His humanistic and inclusive pedagogy is relevant to the experiences of the oppressed, advocating for a critical consciousness as a prerequisite to interrogate oppressive realities and achieve emancipation. However, implementing this framework within national education systems presents challenges. For instance, Freire's model assumes critical consciousness, which I argue develops through encounters that cross boundaries of difference—an assumption that excludes individuals educated in homogeneous national contexts that reinforce the same ideologies. Such environments restrict exposure to the dialectics of the local and the global, limiting opportunities for critical interrogation of the status quo.

On the other hand, Bourdieu's analysis of cultural and social reproduction identifies top-down, prescribed content as symbolic violence that produces "habitus." While insightful, his theory leaves critical questions unanswered: Can all forms of habitus be deemed negative? Who determines what constitutes a "good" habitus? How can we reconcile universal cultural values with local specificities when conflicts arise? These gaps invite further inquiry into the nuanced ways individuals and systems negotiate these tensions.

A promising avenue for future research is the feasibility of implementing Freire's pedagogy in conservative or authoritarian contexts to empower teachers and learners. While symbolic violence often defines such settings, forms of resistance and agency also emerge. This raises critical questions: How do teachers and learners in these contexts exercise their agency to challenge dominant narratives? Do teachers engage critically with the materials they are given, and if so, what alternative resources or strategies do they employ? What systemic or cultural barriers inhibit such critical reflection?

These questions pave the way for the subsequent chapters of this edited volume, which explore the following themes: Freire's influences in place-based learning, ecopedagogy, the culture of silence, inclusive classrooms, counter-storytelling, critical pedagogy, and Theater of the Oppressed. Together, these themes examine the transformative potential of education as a site of resistance and empowerment.

Notes

1   "By 2030 ensure all learners acquire knowledge and skills needed to promote sustainable development, including among others through education for sustainable development and sustainable lifestyles, human rights, gender equality, promotion of a culture of peace and non-violence, global citizenship, and appreciation of cultural diversity and of culture's contribution to sustainable development" (UNESCO, 2015).

2   An example would include the competency-based reforms of 2003 and the Bologna Process in Algeria.

3   I define empowerment as the outcome of education that equips both educators and learners with the knowledge, skills, and attitudes to interrogate, resist, and challenge different forms of oppression. This form of education also allows them to use their agency and work toward the core values of global citizenship: environmental sustainability, peace, and human solidarity.

References

Abdi, A. A., Shultz, L., & Pillay, T. (2015). Decolonizing global citizenship: An introduction. In A. A. Abdi, L. Shultz, & T. Pillay (Eds.), *Decolonizing global citizenship education* (pp. 1–10). Rotterdam: Sense Publishers. https://doi.org/10.1007/978-94-6300-277-6_1.

Al-Newashi, Q. (2012). Images of Europeans in Jordanian textbooks. In S. Alayan, A. Rohde, & S. Dhouib (Eds.), *The politics of education reform in the Middle East: Self and other in textbooks and curricula* (pp. 194–208). New York, NY: Berghahn books.

Andreotti, V. (2010). Postcolonial and post critical "Global Citizenship Education". In G. Elliott, C. Fourali, & S. Issler (Eds.), *Education and social change: Connecting local and global perspectives* (pp. 238–50). New York, NY, and London: Continuum international publishing group.

Apple, M., & Christian-Smith, L. (Eds.) (1991). *The politics of the textbook*. New York, NY: Routledge.

Apple, W. M. (1993). *Democratic education in a conservative age*. New York, NY: Routledge.

Bishara, A. M. (2020). *EFL pedagogy as cultural discourse: Textbooks, practice, and policy for Arabs and Jews in Israel*. New York, NY: Routledge.

Bourdieu, P. (1989). Social space and symbolic power. *Sociological Theory, 7*(1), 14–25. doi: 10.2307/202060.

Bourdieu, P., & Passeron, J. C. (1970). *La Reproduction: Eléments pour une théorie du système de l'enseignement. Livre I: Fondement d'une théorie de la Violence Symbolique*. Paris: Les éditions de minuit.

Bourdieu, P., Wacquant, L. J. D., & Farage, S. (1994). Rethinking the state: Genesis and structure of the bureaucratic field. *Sociological Theory, 12*(1), 1–18. doi: 10.2307/202032.

Freire, P. (1970). *Pedagogy of the oppressed* (50th Anniversary ed.). New York, NY: Bloomsbury Publishing Inc.

Freire, P. (2005). Education for critical consciousness. New York, NY: Continuum.

GEFI (2012). Global education first initiative: An initiative of the united nations secretary-general. Available: http://www.unesco.org/new/en/gefi/about/.

Green, A. (1990). *Education and state formation: The rise of education systems in England, France and the USA*. London: MacMillan.

Hadjeris, F. (2024). Colourism and indigeneity: The portrayal of Tuareg Amazighs in EFL textbooks in Algeria. *Journal of Curriculum Studies*, 56(5), 626–44.

Harvey, D. (2005). *A brief history of neoliberalism*. New york, NY: Oxford University Press.

Jorgenson, S., & Shultz, L. (2012). Global Citizenship Education (GCE) in post-secondary institutions: What is protected and what is hidden under the umbrella of GCE? *Journal of Global Citizenship & Equity Education*, 2(1), 1–22.

Levinson, A. U. B. (2011). Symbolic domination and the reproduction of inequality. In A. U. B. Levinson, P. K. J. Gross, C. Hanks, H. J. Dadds, D. K. Kumasi, J. Link, & D. Metro-Roland (Eds.), *Beyond critique: Exploring critical social theories and education*. New York, NY: Paradigm publishers.

Piller, I., & Cho, J. (2013). Neoliberalism as language policy. *Language in Society*, 42(1), 23–44.

Sant, E., Davies, I., Pashby, K., & Shultz, L. (2018). *Global citizenship education: A critical introduction to key concepts and debates*. London: Bloomsbury Publishing Plc.

Shultz, L. (2007). Educating for global citizenship: Conflicting agendas and understandings—ProQuest. *Alberta Journal of Educational Research*, 53(3), 248–58.

Tawil, S. (2013). Education for "global citizenship": A framework for discussion. *Education Research and Foresight Working Papers*.

Torres, C. A. (2017). *Theoretical and empirical foundations of critical global citizenship education*. New York, NY: Routledge, Taylor & Francis Group.

Torres, C. A., & Bosio, E. (2020). Global citizenship education at the crossroads: Globalization, global commons, common good, and critical consciousness, 48, 99–113. https://doi.org/10.1007/s11125-019-09458-w.

UNESCO. (2014). *Global citizenship education: Preparing learners for the challenges of the twenty-first century*. UNESCO, May 11. https://www.unesco.org/en/articles/global-citizenship-education-preparing-learners-challenges-twenty-first-century.

UNESCO (2015). *Global citizenship education: Topics and learning objectives*.

UNESCO (2018). *Preparing teachers for global citizenship education: A template.* UNESCO.

Wiseman, W. A. (2014). Representations of Islam and Arab societies in western secondary textbooks, PhD Lehigh University. *Digest of Middle East Studies*, 23(2), 312–44.

CHAPTER TWO

Grown from the "Concrete": Engaging Freire and Place-Based Learning Inquiry

Brian Zamora

In the discourse that spans critical pedagogy, the role of concrete conditions has played an integral role as an incubating site for teaching and learning. For Peter McLaren (2015), the relationship between learning and these concrete conditions was made apparent in a conversation with Freire. During this exchange, Freire encouraged McLaren to "translate his work within the contextual specificity of where [McLaren] was standing—where [he] was located—as a teacher and where [his] students were located as students" (p. 243). Freire understood this location as a pedagogical one whose conditions were ripe for learning to emerge.

Notably, the language that Freire draws on to describe these conditions provides a generative frame to understand how critical place inquiry is conducive to an analysis of learning. There is a conceptual landscape at our disposal that emerges when we align Freire's language to place-based social practices, more broadly. At its heart, a place-centered learning practice foregrounds the local as the location by which concrete and social conditions produce learning. The shared knowledge base provided by this foundation affords a social, place-based disposition for people to more fully participate as learners in their communities. This view encourages us, in our social-educational inquiries, to look more intentionally into the place-based learning systems inherent in the racialized communities with and for whom we work. In this light, we

FIGURE 2.1 *Walkways on San Fernando Road— Sylmar, CA.*

use this view to raise the following: How might centering place-based learning in critical social inquiry help develop the conditions for social praxis?

In this chapter, I respond to Vossoughi and Gutierrez's (2016) call for "further inquiry into the forms of critical social consciousness *already present* in the communities" to address the significance of centering place for social inquiry (p. 155, emphasis added). Specifically, I consider how both critical pedagogy and critical place inquiry embrace social practices to interrogate how people in racialized communities embrace learning. I begin by outlining literature that explores how critical place inquiry can establish a foundation for learning through the research inquiries it pursues. I introduce *social practices* to understand how learning is located in the pedagogical engagements between persons and the places they interact with most closely. Then, I reflect on the insights that this emphasis on critical place inquiry can have for learning practices involving learning and place. I conclude by sharing a case study that explores how learning through a place-based frame emerges in an online class on Indigenous identity for urban Chicanx youth.

Critical Place Inquiry

Social practices draw on a unique emphasis of the everyday practices that arise through place (Kusenbach, 2020; Pink, 2012). An analysis of learning through the frame of place can bear fruit to important cultural insights produced when they are situated in the everyday (Lave, 2019). Freire sought to engage this situatedness through the "starting point," a concept "from which [learners'] epistemological curiosity will work to produce a more critically scientific knowledge" (1998, p. 62). There is an opening by which place can shine light on the social practices for research inquiries in education that centers learning. As Freire contends, "It's impossible to talk of respect for students ... without taking into consideration the conditions in which they are living" (p. 62). Freire makes clear that the ways in which place is studied has implications for our understandings of learning. Education scholars have similarly called attention to the gradual emergence of place in education (Tuck & McKenzie, 2015). Butler and Sinclair's review of education research, for instance, reviewed studies in education whose research on place inquiry and spatial methods spanned "any form of empirical research that collects place-specific data, draws on these data explicitly during data analysis, and/or generates insights that speak back to the role of place" (2020, p. 70). Notably, this review does not identify place-based learning practices in the scope of their review. Freire makes clear that learning arises precisely because of the place-based conditions that make it possible. The observation from Butler and Sinclair that the studies in their review "do not necessarily collect data specific to the places they are studying, [or] consider the impact of local contexts in their analysis" (p. 71) should, therefore, be a commitment to take seriously the role of place in our inquiries.

The implications that emerge from these conceptions of place invite a discussion about how critical pedagogy and critical place inquiry can be used to engage learning practices. Broadly, critical place inquiry encompasses methodologies whose situated, conceptual focus on place engages educational contexts and learning conditions, whereas critical pedagogy foregrounds the social conditions that influence the learning encounter.

Critical Place Inquiry

Research methodologies whose emerging epistemologies, social practices, and meanings are immersed within place by which to make meaning of the world.

This dialog draws on previous dialogs from Tuck and McKenzie (2015), who frame critical place inquiry as "research that takes up critical questions and develops corresponding methodological approaches … in responding to critical place issues such as those of globalization and neoliberalism, settler colonialism, and environmental degradation" (p. 2).

Into the Starting Point

For Paulo Freire, learning processes are produced organically from the everyday forms of inquiry that emerge in community contexts. Freire identified these practices as ingenuous—forms of learning that are produced organically from open, everyday forms. The significance of these contexts arose from the proximity by which learners gained an awareness of their concrete conditions, which Freire contended should be built on to embody a more scientific form. This contention has been a source of contention for sociocultural thinkers like Vossoughi and Gutierrez, who argue that this distinction "suggests that everyday forms of knowing/asking are somehow less epistemological" (Vossoughi and Gutierrez, 2016, p. 155). To affirm the epistemic frames—ways of knowing—that learners draw from is to simultaneously affirm the places from which these arise. Subsequently, it makes sense that discussions surrounding learning practices should engage place in the same regard that critical place inquiry are held to, as well.

Where place was most closely embraced by Freire was through the conceptualization of the starting point. Identifying the social conditions of learning was fundamental for Freire because it identified the point of pedagogical encounter: the point in which the landscape of learning is located. The significance of these starting points was most evident through continuous reflections upon his own teaching practice in his book *Pedagogy of Freedom* (1998):

The more my own practice as a teacher increases in methodological rigor, the more respect I must have for the ingenuous knowledge of the student. For this ingenuous knowledge is the starting point from which his/her epistemological curiosity will work to produce a more critically scientific knowledge.

(p. 62)

Within his later works such as the above, there is evidence of an emerging analysis toward the study of how learning processes themselves are based in—and influence—place. By identifying the intellectual location of the learner, he identifies his own location as an educator. These observations resonate with those of Tuck and McKenzie, who call for the study of place to better understand "how we do inquiry and research, but also what counts as evidence, as knowing, as legitimacy, as rigorous, as ethical, and as useful" (p. 46). There is a connecting tissue that arises from both of their insights: the importance of situating research (as social practices) alongside place as mutually constitutive themes. Taken together, both sets of social practices command a deep reflection toward place to produce greater insights about the concrete social conditions that are present.

I argue that a methodological approach that uses place to approach learning processes reveals a *nearness* at the learners' disposal in both the spatial and epistemological forms. This nearness, which is emplaced from within the learners' physical and social communities, engages spatial practices toward a critical social consciousness. Theoretical points of similarity between place research and learning, when further researched, enable place as a necessary tool to uncover how—and where—critical pedagogy achieves democratic social praxis.

Praxis[1]

A relational intellectual relationship from the Freirean tradition that locates critical intellectual foundations at the crux of reflection and action.

Critical Pedagogy and Place

Greenwood was amongst the first (2003, 2008) to discuss and theorize a critical pedagogy of place, which paired Freirean thought with an ecological analysis to study the role of spatial environments. Greenwood draws on critical pedagogy to locate consciousness at the disposal of learners through their own ingenuous curiosity (Freire, 2018). Similar to Freire's starting point, Greenwood engages social contexts to make inferences about where critical consciousness emerges from. By drawing on shared points between place and place-based education, Greenwood outlines that a *critical pedagogy of place* is focused primarily on a political call to study the location of education itself, as opposed to asking how learning is engaged in these locations.

While Greenwood establishes that the bounds of the starting point can be a fruitful location for critical reflection, he does not address Freire's insistence on moving away from that original place for a scientific knowledge. In Freire's (1998) words:

Its epistemological "distance" from practice as an object of analysis ought to be compensated for by an even greater proximity to the object of analysis, in terms of lived experience. The better this process is accomplished, the greater is the … communicability in overcoming an ingenuous attitude toward knowledge.

(p. 44)

Critical pedagogy of place

Aims to (a) identify, recover, and create material spaces and places that teach us how to live well in our total environments (reinhabitation); and (b) identify and change ways of thinking that injure and exploit other people and places (decolonization). (2003, p. 9)

For Freire, there is an additional frame of analysis needed in addition to place alone—one of learning—to understand the role of learning processes within place without "overcoming" the starting point. Based on Freire's elaborations, it is unclear whether critical reflection can take place from within the starting point: "through reflection on a given practice, ingenuous curiosity must perceive itself as such so as to advance to the critical stage" (p. 43).

Building on these ideas presented by Greenwood and Freire, I posit that this critical outlook *can* be gained from the place it was first conceived. Freire contends that a generative learning practice is made possible for people when critical reflection is at their disposal. Place, particularly when it is studied alongside the epistemic subject positions of racialized groups, is itself a generative engagement for both ingenuous knowledge and critical reflection to flourish. The role of place should be fundamental to any dialog surrounding learning concerned with starting points. Indeed, place is not a mere analytic frame by which to supplement discussions on learning: it has a specific agency of its own that must be affirmed for a critical line of research. It is just as sound a methodological practice to analyze learning by looking inward, not just outside the concrete conditions. There is a *nearness* to place that details the significance of how and why to conduct research with place in mind. As Meyer (2008) writes:

> You came from a place. You grew in a place and you had a relationship with that place. *This is an epistemological idea* … One does not simply learn about land, we learn best *from* land. This knowing makes you *intelligent* to my people. How you are on land or in the ocean tells us something about you. *Absolutely.* It opens doors to the specificity of what it means to exist in a space and how that existing extends into how best to interact in it.
>
> (p. 217, emphasis original)

Meyer's insights emphasize that Land plays a fundamental role to learning through the agentic disposition it provides

FIGURE 2.2 *Virgen de San Fer—San Fernando, CA.*

for people (Tuck & McKenzie, 2015). This epistemic idea, as Meyer poses, points directly to the agency that Land asserts for persons to exist, move, and learn with. We can consider this conceptualization as a transition to the case study below.

Place and Learning, Enacted

To elaborate on learning and its nearness to place, I present select data from a case study conducted in the summer of 2020 in a class on Indigenous identity from a bookstore and cultural center in a Latinx-majority neighborhood in Southern California. This class was composed of three Chicana/x identifying students and two instructors; I served as participant observer. My role as a lifelong community member provided me with an insider position toward some of the social practices engaged. Since this course took place at the height of the Covid-19 pandemic, the classes took place virtually through Zoom. This course format demanded the class draw even more closely on place by engaging learning processes whose *nearness* to the students produced ideal starting points that directly connected with them. The instructors also introduced several guest speakers whose careers were engaged directly with dialogs on place-based traditions and Indigenous identity. The guest speakers were invited to present to the course following student requests to learn more about specific Indigenous (Mexica) practices and histories. These guest speakers usually responded to questions given ahead of time to them by participants. The questions prompted to them were the following:

1   How did you get in touch with your Indigenous identity?
2   How has this Indigenous identity flourished in your career paths?

As community members central to the city and cultural foundations from which the course drew from, I understand the guest speakers' reflections as complementary to—and representative of—the class theme of what it means to be an Indigenous person. The following excerpts demonstrate their perceptions of being in place through reflections shared to the youth in a learning setting. I comment on their context and the emerging insights about place and learning.

Lucy is a Huichol and Chicana guest speaker whose centrality of her Indigenous identity to her career as a social worker and an education program manager for the Tataviam Fernandeño Band of Mission Indians. Throughout her contributions, Lucy shares how her reconnection as an Indigenous woman unfolded from her first memories as a child into her professional adulthood years. Her knowledge base in the community engages her understanding of where learning processes are located even more closely through her contributions during a reflection session known as *palabra*, or "word":

Lucy: And I know there is a lot that I left out, but I just want to tell you, even though you hear the same information, I just want to kind of go back on what Melissa was saying. Every time we hear each other speak, we get new information. That's usually because we develop in different places, and it will take on a new meaning. So, be gentle with yourselves, know that you have a community. Know that you are here and we see you and you matter and you have a community behind you. And I say that because the very same community that you're in right now, was there for me when I was 17.

From the first meeting, it was customary for the class to participate in a reflection period in which all members would share their main takeaways and feelings associated to the class in a period known as "sharing palabra," or *sharing the word*. This closing provided a period for personal narratives to be shared in a horizontal fashion between everyone involved in the class, including course instructors and guests. Lucy palabra encompasses an embrace of social meanings, rooted in place to understand how we center our learning customs. This multiplicity of learning reveals a shared intimacy and curiosity bound by a common location. Her relationship to the bookstore adds another dimension of encouragement to the students in the class invested in finding a channel by which to learn more about their Indigenous roots.

In a career like social work that mandates closely knit community relations, Lucy reveals how different communities produce their own unique, nuanced learning processes. Similarly, the resonance these places provide to the class is something Maria, an elder from the bookstore, concretizes by sharing how these physical places have tangible impacts for learning:

He already knew that the Martinez family on the reservation, because he was working with youth there, because he was

FIGURE 2.3 *Liquor Corner Store—San Fernando, CA.*

part of a program that he developed to try to get youth back in connection with nature, and he would take them on a lot of hikes up into the mountains. And basically, reconnecting with one of the things that has been taken away from us in a lot of ways, and that is our connection to nature. And he would find that when they were out there, they would be more likely to sit in circle, to share their stories and just not be distracted like in the many ways that we are sometimes when we are in the city.

By being in nature, participants expressed new insights they made about their histories and connections with culture. To sit in a circle, Maria understands, is more than a pedagogical tool, but an epistemological one as well. Moreover, Maria perceives this reconnection with nature as a renewed one, thereby affirming the role of place in their capacity to learn in a relational fashion.

Conclusion

Critical place inquiry supports learning practices by studying the places from which they blossom. One of the major

FIGURE 2.4 *Overlooking the Northeast Valley—Sylmar, CA.*

commitments this chapter makes is the importance of the social practices already in place. By aligning learning to the social practices it is situated in, we can locate place in the purview of critical pedagogy itself. Future engagements with critical place inquiry should envision methodological interventions that weave on-the-ground forms of learning. Such a research design is directly in line with Freirean calls for racialized groups to see the word and the world through literacy. This is also in line with Indigenous traditions with a horizontal worldview of learning and conviviality. I call for future research whose commitments to place foregrounds learning alongside, and already present, in the community.

Note

1   Praxis is a dialectical intellectual concept inherited from a broader Marxist tradition in which critical thought informs a response to social and material conditions. Critical pedagogy centers praxis in education to consider how classed and racialized people can transform these conditions by using literacy to affirm their relation to the world. Critical pedagogues like Antonia Darder and Henry Giroux have both extended praxis to analyze dominant ideologies in education and the role of linguistically diverse learners to engage in the world, respectively.

References

Agnew, J. (1987). *Place and politics: The geographical mediation of state and society*. London: Allen & Unwin.

Butler, A., & Sinclair, K. A. (2020). Place matters: A critical review of place inquiry and spatial methods in education research. *Review of Research in Education*, 44(1), 64–96.

Carpenter, S., & Mojab, S. (2017). *Revolutionary learning: Marxism, feminism and knowledge*. London: Pluto Press.

Darder, A. (2012). *Culture and power in the classroom: Educational foundations for the schooling of bicultural students* (2nd ed.). New York, NY: Routledge.

Darder, A. (Ed.) (2019). *Decolonizing interpretive research: A subaltern methodology for social change* (1st ed.). London: Routledge.

Freire, P. (1973). *Education for critical consciousness*. New York, NY: Seabury Press.

Freire, P. (1993). *Pedagogy of the city*. New York, NY: Continuum.

Freire, P. (1994). *Pedagogy of hope*. New York, NY: Continuum.

Freire, P. (1998). *Pedagogy of freedom: Ethics, democracy, and civic courage*. Lanham, MD: Rowman & Littlefield Publishers.

Freire, P. (2018). *Pedagogy of the oppressed* (50th anniversary ed.). New York, NY: Bloomsbury Academic.

Greenwood, D. A. (2008). A critical pedagogy of place: From gridlock to parallax. *Environmental Education Research*, 14(3), 336–48.

Greenwood, D. A. (2013). A critical theory of place-conscious education. In R. B. Stevenson, M. Brody, J. Dillon, & A. E. J. Wals (Eds.), *International handbook of research on environmental education* (1st ed.) (pp. 93–100). New York, NY: Routledge. https://doi.org/10.4324/9780203813331.

Gruenewald (2003). The best of both worlds: A critical pedagogy of place. *Educational Researcher*, 32(4), 3–12.

Kusenbach, M. (2020). Mobile methods. In M. R. M. Ward (Ed.), *Handbook of qualitative research in education* (2nd ed.) (pp. 257–69). Cheltenham: Edward Elgar Publishing.

Lave, J. (2019). *Learning and everyday life: Access, participation, and changing practice*. Berkeley, CA: Cambridge University Press. https://doi.org/10.1017/9781108616416.

Marin, A., Taylor, K. H., Shapiro, B. R., & Hall, R. (2020). Why learning on the move: Intersecting research pathways for mobility, learning and teaching. *Cognition and Instruction*, 38(3), 265–80.

Mayo, P. (2005). *Education for radical humanization in neoliberal times: A review of Paulo Freire's later work*. Lanham, MD: Rowman & Littlefield.

McKenzie, M., & Tuck, E. (2015). *Place in research: Theory, methodology, and methods*.

McLaren, P. (2015). *Life in schools: An introduction to critical pedagogy in the foundations of education* (6th ed.). Routledge.

McLaren, P. (2016). *Pedagogy of insurrection: From resurrection to revolution*. New York, NY: Peter Lang.

Meyer, M. (2008). Indigenous and authentic: Hawaiian epistemology and the triangulation of meaning. In N. K. Denzin, Y. S. Lincoln, & L. T. Smith (Eds.), *Handbook of critical and indigenous methodologies* (pp. 217–32). Los Angeles, CA; London: SAGE Publications, Inc.

Paris, D. (2012). Culturally sustaining pedagogy: A needed change in stance, terminology, and practice. *Educational Researcher*, 41(3), 93–7.

Paris, D., & Alim, H. S. (Eds.) (2017). *Culturally sustaining pedagogies: Teaching and learning for justice in a changing world*. New York, NY: Teachers College Press.

Pink, S. (2012). *Situating everyday life: Practices and places*. London: SAGE.

Rodriguez, L. (2020). *From our land to our land: Essays, journeys, and imaginings from a native Xicanx writer*. New York, NY: Seven Stories Press.

Tuck, E., & McKenzie, M. (2014). *Place in research: Theory, methodology, and methods*. London: Taylor and Francis.

Vossoughi, S., & Gutiérrez, K. D. (2016). Critical pedagogy and sociocultural theory. In I. Esmonde, & A. N. Booker (Eds.), *Power and privilege in the learning sciences: Critical and sociocultural theories of learning* (1st ed.) (pp. 139–61). Taylor and Francis. https://doi.org/10.4324/9781315685762.

Zavala, M. (2018). *Raza struggle and the movement for ethnic studies: Decolonial pedagogies, literacies, and methodologies* (Education and struggle, v. 17). New York, NY: Peter Lang. doi: 10.3726/b14435.

CHAPTER THREE

The Inclusive Classroom: A Path to Praxis for LGBTQ+ Educators and Students in Response to Rising School-Based Censorship and Exclusion

Darek Ciszek

US states have proposed, and in some cases implemented, controversial "don't say gay" laws across schools in recent years. Many of the bills broadly and ambiguously prohibit discussion of sexual orientation and gender identity in curriculum and instruction (ACLU, 2024). These education policies present profound challenges to teachers' and students' academic freedom and the creation of safe, welcoming classrooms. Few could have imagined such laws passing in any state legislature. Consequently, educators see LGBTQ-inclusive curricular policies as needed more than ever to stem the tide of discrimination and promote inclusion in our nation's schools.

Instead of censorship, educators need instructional models that reflect the lives of *all* their students. Accordingly, I draw on Paulo Freire's *Pedagogy of the Oppressed* to discuss the critical need to align curriculum and instruction with students' actual experiences. In particular, I posit that we stand to learn from Freire's focus on dialogical forms of pedagogical practice and raising students' awareness of their oppression or engaging in *conscientization*.

However, because Freire never directly took up the issue of LGBTQ-inclusive education, his ideas warrant a broader extension for the current project. Specifically, I propose that combining Freire's foundational ideas alongside a discussion of critical content analysis and queer pedagogy helps us examine the broader social and power-based context in which LGBTQ lives are censored in schools. Such an amalgamated approach builds on Freire's insights and furthers the scholarship in LGBTQ-inclusive education by speaking to forms of power and control in curriculum and instruction. Indeed, at its core, LGBTQ-inclusive education challenges *heteronormative* forms of instruction, and accordingly, dominant ways of knowing the world and ways of existing in the world that alienate and demean queer people.

Freire's Banking Model of Education

We first review the seminal work of Paulo Freire (1970) and his theory of the banking model of education, which is often used to discuss capitalism's role in schooling and social reproduction. However, I posit that there is more to glean from Freire's most novel theory of education when applied to the *heteronormative* nature of K-12 schooling, which I define as the *social reproduction of heterosexuality and a cisgender identity as the only viable options for establishing meaningful human relationships and self-identity*. Following the banking model, Freire argues that students are seen as mere accounts into which teachers "deposit" information meant to be studied, memorized, and ultimately tested. Freire states: "*The more completely she fills the receptacles, the better a teacher she is. The more meekly the receptacles permit themselves to be filled, the better students they are ... this is the banking model of education, in which the scope of action allowed to the students extends only as far as receiving, filing, and storing deposits*" (Freire, 1970, p. 72, italics mine). Thus, in applying the banking model, we can likewise situate LGBTQ students (and their allies) as lacking agency in classrooms. Simply stated, queer students do not get the chance to see themselves reflected in their learning environments because of a dominant, heteronormative curriculum. Similarly, teachers who (un) wittingly subscribe to this model position LGBTQ identities and experiences as illicit.

The information that students are "deposited" represents dominant heterosexual and cisgender ways of knowing and ways of being. Teachers are commended for making these deposits without question, and students are marked for compliance as they "meekly" accept the knowledge as societal and historical truth. In other words, there are no alternatives to being heterosexual and cisgender. If a teacher's classroom has queer or questioning students, they do not benefit from any self, or possible future self, representation. While Freire does not directly comment on the experience of LGBTQ youth in schools, what is important to note are the instructional policies that use power to enforce (any) form of authoritative knowledge; this is the core insight from Freire's banking model. Policymakers, school leaders, and educators who reinforce heteronormative curricular and pedagogical practices can be compared to Freire's oppressors as they engage in the school-based social reproduction of an exclusively heterosexual and cisgender society that, at best, makes queer lives irrelevant and invisible, and at worst, constructs them as criminal.

Yet, Freire also offers pedagogical solutions. Namely, his theory of education is grounded in the dialog between teachers and students and emphasizes the need to raise students' awareness of their current state or *conscientization* (see Figure 3.1). Following this instructional approach, students come to a critical understanding of societal structures through teacher-guided reflection. In the process, students explore the root causes of their alienation as sexual or gender minorities, and look for ways to change their circumstances, or engage in *praxis,* which is an application of their learning to empower themselves (Freire, 1970). Following an LGBTQ-inclusive educational model, teachers present students with representative content that includes information about the LGBTQ community, historically (e.g., Gay Liberation and Civil Rights) and contemporaneously (e.g., the struggle for same-sex marriage). Notably, the process includes dialog, with students able to share their own experience of being queer, questioning, or an ally. Academic subjects can also vary, such as a history class or for younger grades, ensuring students from same-gender caregiver households are represented and can discuss their families openly (e.g., two moms or dads). Examples abound and are not limited to specific grade levels or subject areas.

FIGURE 3.1 *A dialogical approach to LGBTQ-inclusive education.*

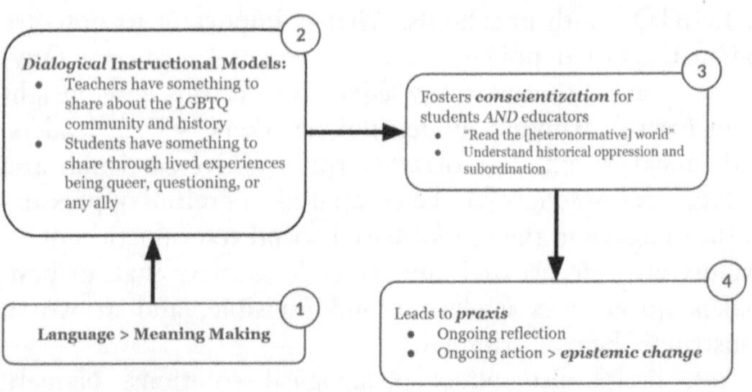

Note. This figure is original fand was created by the author based on a synthesis of literature.

Moreover, a dialogical approach to pedagogy is one of the foundational concepts underpinning Freirean philosophy (Figure 3.1, step 1). According to such a model, and to the extent possible, curriculum and instruction are organized from a *student's point of view*. In this sense, liberated from a biased and authoritative curriculum set down by a biased state apparatus, teachers and students see education as generative, something fostered in the classroom through critical and creative processes in a mutual exchange of personal experiences and knowledge. Such an instructional approach also means that students must be trusted to connect classroom material to their own lives. Teachers begin to see that their students have legitimate experiences; pedagogy becomes co-intentional with the power to create and re-create new forms of knowledge between teacher and student (Freire, 1970). In our present case, students learn about queer communities, and teachers get an opportunity to learn from queer, questioning, or allied youth (Figure 3.1, step 2). In the process, teachers contest heteronormative structures that would otherwise silence them and their students. Indeed, challenging heteronormativity's power over traditional schooling (Figure 3.1, step 3) through a dialogical learning approach can help learners achieve praxis that is rooted in *epistemic change*, or the reevaluation of what constitutes "legitimate" human knowledge and experience (Figure 3.1, step 4).

The Heteronormative Mindset and Expanding on Freire's Model of Change

Paulo Freire has much to contribute to how we think about authoritative models of education. As the earlier section argues, his philosophy of education can be extended to LGBTQ-inclusive education. In doing so, we begin to think about how Freire's work applies to historically novel situations and student populations he never considered. Thus, I strive to

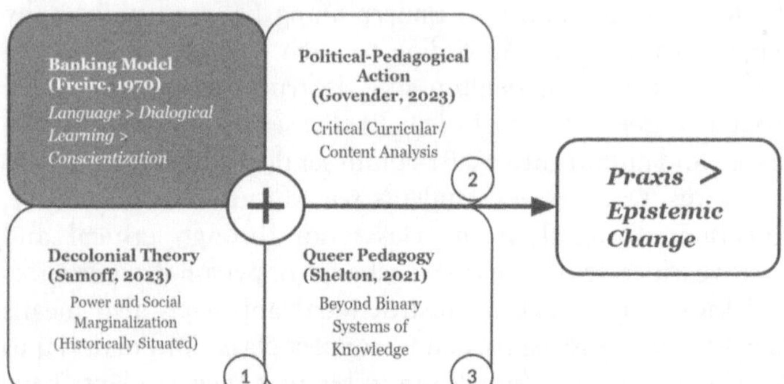

Note. This Figure is original and was created by the author based on a synthesis of literature.

build on his work by incorporating relevant theories of power and pedagogy, each having distinctive and additive value for situating LGBTQ-inclusive education in a *praxis*-oriented context (Figure 3.2).

Decolonial Theory

Looking at restrictions toward LGBTQ-inclusive education from an epistemic *and* colonial perspective allows us to unpack how dominant relational and gendered social norms shape and influence curriculum and instruction (Figure 3.2, step 1). In particular, what follows is a review of what is arguably at the core of the resistance to queer-inclusive education: reproducing heteronormativity. According to the extant literature, through colonial paradigms, nations have a history of oppressing minority groups and engaging in cultural control through schooling systems (Samoff, 2023). Similarly, and building on Freire's notion of conscientization, I propose that adopting a decolonial mindset helps us see how heteronormativity, as a *forced social and cultural experience*, is deeply problematic for those who understand and live different sexual and gendered lives (Grosfoguel, 2007).

Moreover, when it comes to teaching, educators often have tunnel vision around diversity, inclusivity, and intersectionality (Samoff, 2023). The narrow scope is due, in part, to the culturally biased training, resources, and curricular exposure teachers receive as part of their formal training. This tunnel vision must end if we are to engage in a liberatory, *praxis*-oriented education. If successful in the context of LGBTQ-inclusive education, educators would see the controlling role heteronormativity plays in shaping teachers' and students' experiences and the deep tensions it creates for curriculum and instructional design. Additionally, Samoff argues that anticolonial activists "understood the necessity of decolonizing the colonial mind" (Samoff, 2023, p. 60). Again, in adopting a decolonial framework, we should push ourselves to challenge the "heteronormative mind" as something power-based, even imperial, concerning those individuals who inherently do not conform to dominant sexual and gender-based norms.

Accordingly, what is happening in many states across the US is symbolic of a much larger struggle for creating safe spaces that honor diversity and challenge heteronormativity in classrooms. Schools that wish to implement LGBTQ-affirming instructional strategies will, inevitably, need to grapple with the extent to which heteronormativity has historically shaped curriculum and teachers' and students' taken-for-granted approaches to teaching and learning. Borrowing from Samoff and building on Freire's conscientization, decolonial theory proves instructive for educators as it considers how social norms and power may be used to analyze heteronormativity and its marginalization of sexual and gender identities. In line with Freire's oppressors (Freire, 1970), educators and students begin to see how LGBTQ people become "othered" in ways that disenfranchise them relative to a more prevailing and legally protected heterosexual and cisgender majority. Indeed, this process begins in school as heterosexuality and a cisgender identity are exclusively normalized through a biased curriculum that does not acknowledge the humanity and life experiences of queer people.

Political-Pedagogical Action

What information is included and how it is used to create the conditions for interaction with and among students underscore the political nature of curriculum and instruction. Govender (2023) draws on critical pedagogy and decolonial theory to question how curriculum is often presented as universal by dominant power groups. He argues that such universalism is inherently colonial, "Universality … is a colonial device for positioning certain knowledge, cultures, languages, cis-gendered norms, heteronormativities, and other social categories as original and timeless" (Govender, 2023, p. 239). Accordingly, by suppressing queer lives, heteronormative school policies create the impression that heterosexual and cisgender identities are uniquely valid. These identities are further positioned as "timeless" as censorship also precludes the teaching of queer histories, some going back centuries. Past and present examples of queer people are crucially important for LGBTQ youth who may feel their existence is without precedence; nothing could be further from the truth (Butler, 1993).

In line with Freire's emphasis on dialogical forms of learning, Govender offers a way for educators to critically engage their classroom-based practices through *political-pedagogical action* (Figure 3.2, step 2). His stance on pedagogy is anticolonial and stresses how educators' decisions, from content selection to instruction, are "bound to power" (Govender, 2023, p. 236). Moreover, he argues that political-pedagogical action allows "teachers [to make] pedagogical choices in more socially just ways that empower themselves and students to deconstruct and reconstruct teaching and learning in more equitable ways" (Govender, 2023, p. 236).

This is accomplished by putting social plurality at the center of pedagogical practice, directly challenging heteronormative power. Students and teachers incorporate their diverse backgrounds as artifacts for learning and meaning-making. Ultimately, the instructional approach critically examines subject content and calls on students to ask more profound questions (Govender, 2023). *Who is included vs excluded in these texts? What dominant narratives are represented? And how are social and political issues or histories embedded in this topic?* In short, teachers equip their students with information that could shape their lives for the better, especially if they are part of a minority, and learn how to engage in ongoing reflective action regarding their social, political, and cultural position in a society.

Queer Pedagogy: Beyond Binary Structures

Queer pedagogy stems from queer theory and challenges binary systems in education (Figure 3.2, step 3). Shelton (2021) defines "queer" as that "which refers broadly not only to lesbian, gay, bisexual, [or] trans students but to any students who self-identify beyond binary conceptions of gender and sexualities" (Shelton, 2021, p. 1). By extension, queer pedagogy gives teachers and students a space to "problematize the ways social structures such as schools normalize and enforce particular language and behaviors" that extend heterosexuality as the assumed, and indeed compulsory, norm (Shelton, 2021, p. 5). Furthermore, Planella-Ribera et al. (2020) point out that sexual identities are historically and socially constructed and that attempting to "fix" them is a form of social control. Queer pedagogy actively resists such influence and allows educators and students to notice and challenge the social conventions that underpin formal schooling (Planella-Ribera et al., 2020, p. 240). In some ways, queer pedagogy can be thought of as an extension of Freire's core principles albeit for a marginalized student and educator population he never studied.

Queering the curriculum extends beyond a focus on the lived experiences of queer students. Indeed, because a queer pedagogical approach challenges *all* binary ways of knowing and ways of being, all students that do not fit into the binary ideological order stand to benefit (Mattheis et al., 2021). That order includes students of color, immigrant/ migrant students, and students with disabilities (e.g., ableism). Hence, a queer approach to curriculum disrupts normative thinking by questioning what is socially expected and acceptable. Historically, American school curricula were primarily crafted from the point of view of white, heterosexual, cisgender, and male Western Europeans. Academic standards were not, and still are not, fully representative of America's diverse student population (Goldstein, 2014). From a Freirean and queer standpoint, these academic expectations must be challenged as they do not sufficiently consider the experiences of all students and their educators (Anzaldúa, 2012).

Furthermore, there has been a long-held assumption in schools that students and their family members are heterosexual and cisgender by *default*. Yet due to the strides made by the LGBTQ rights movement in recent decades, marriage equality in 2015 being a notable example, such assumptions are finally being exposed as false. While much may still appear bleak and there is indeed cause for concern, we can also adopt a cautious optimism as heteronormative school structures are challenged with a focus on inclusion. By adopting a queer pedagogical mindset, we also aim to avoid the perils of binary forms of social knowledge, including instructional standards and techniques that can easily alienate students that do not fit into dominant groups. Indeed, one of the more salient aspects of queer theory is that it has broader application beyond the LGBTQ community when we consider how institutional structures can divide and categorize us all.

Concluding Thoughts

Anti-LGBTQ policies have deeply impacted queer teachers, school leaders, youth, and straight allies. From a Freirean standpoint, LGBTQ-inclusive education means rethinking *how* educators approach teacher–student relationships (i.e., through dialog) and pedagogy to stem the tide of homophobia, transphobia, and biphobia present in American schools. Ultimately, this means challenging heteronormativity in curriculum and instruction. In particular, decolonial theory and queer pedagogy may prove constructive for challenging binary systems of power and exclusion not just for LGBTQ youth but all students who do not fit into established social categories. At the same time, political-pedagogical action offers educators a way to critically examine curricular content that presents students with accepted social and historical "truths." When combined together, these frameworks help us expand on Freire's notion of *praxis* and offer a new approach that educators and policymakers can use to critically examine systems of power. In doing so, we explore commonly erased forms of knowledge and human experience that better match the sheer diversity of humanity. For success, we as a society must also be willing to learn from and respect queer ways of knowing and ways of being.

References

American Civil Liberties Union (ACLU) (2024). "Mapping attacks on LGBTQ rights in U.S," state legislatures in 2024. https://www.aclu.org/map/mapping-attacks-lgbtq-rights-us-state-legislatures-2024.

Anzaldúa, G. (2012). *Borderlands/ La Frontera: The new Mestiza* (4th ed.) San Francisco, CA: Aunt Lute Books.

Butler, J. (1993). Imitation and gender insubordination. In H. Abelove, M. A. Barale, & D. M. Halperin (Eds.), *The lesbian and gay studies reader* (pp. 307–20). New York, NY: Routledge. Print.

Freire, P. (1970). *Pedagogy of the oppressed*. New York, NY: Bloomsbury Publishing.

Freire, P. (2000). *Pedagogy of freedom: Ethics, democracy, and civic courage* (Critical perspectives series: A book series dedicated to Paulo Freire). Lanham, MD, Boulder, CO, New York, NY, and Oxford: Rowman & Littlefield Publishers.

Goldstein, D. (2014). *Teacher wars: A history of America's most embattled profession*. New York, NY: Doubleday Publishing.

Govender, N. (2023). Critical literacies and the conditions of decolonial possibility. In I. Rivers, & C. L. Lovin (Eds.), *Young people shaping democratic politics: Interrogating inclusion, mobilising education* (pp. 235–60). London: Palgrave Macmillan. doi: 10.1007/978-3-031-29378-8_11.

Grosfoguel, R. (2007). The epistemic decolonial turn. *Cultural Studies*, 21(2–3), 211–23. doi: 10.1080/09502380601162514.

Mattheis, A., Lovos, J., Humphrey, C., Eichenberger, L., & Nazar, C. R. (2021). Queering the common core (and the NGSS): Challenging normativity and embracing possibility. *Journal of Homosexuality*, 69(12), 2007–26. doi: 10.1080/00918369.2021.1987748.

Planella-Ribera, J., Pie-Balaguer, A., & Gil-Rodriguez, E. (2020). Technology and queer education: Subversions and educational resistances. *Indian Journal of Gender Studies*, 27(2), 226–41. SAGE. doi: 10.1177/0971521520910965.

Samoff, J. (2023). Institutionalizing international influence. In C. A. Torres, R. F. Arnove, & Lauren I. Misiaszek (Eds.), *Comparative education: The dialectics of the global and the local* (5th ed.) (pp. 29–70). Lanham, MD: Rowman & Littlefield Publishing Group.

Shelton, S. A. (2021). Queer contemplative pedagogy: Challenging gender and sexuality norms through contemplation. *Journal of Homosexuality*, 69(12), 2049–65. doi: 10.1080/00918369.2021.1984789.

CHAPTER FOUR

The "Limit-Situation" and "Culture of Silence": Using Freirean Dialogs to Overcome the Impasse in American P-12 Education

Monte J. Joffee,
Sara A. Tirschwell, T. Willard Fair
and Tai Abrams

This is a fictional instructional manual written to make-believe students as an exercise in imagining Freirean ideas being applied to the most fundamental and practical issue: P-12 national school reform.

Dear high school students:

Do you want to change American P-12 education for yourselves, friends, and siblings? Here we will prepare you for three steps of activism based on two ideas of Paulo Freire: the "limit-situation" and the "culture of silence" (Freire, 2018; Freire, 1985).[1,2] In his work teaching literacy, Freire engaged in deep dialogs to raise what he called "*conscientização*" about education. Consider this chapter as a step-by-step guide to help you engage in "Freirean dialogs" to awaken public *conscientização* about education:

- Step 1: We are asking you to attend local school board meetings and raise thought-provoking questions.
  In so doing, you will break through the headlock of disastrous educational policies that paralyze our schools. Only then will it become possible for fresh ideas to emerge.

- Step 2: We implore you to start conversations about P-12 education with your parents and/or other family members, your teachers, fellow students, and informal leaders in your communities.

- Step 3: Help bring P-12 school reform to the national stage. Let's find "champion" politicians who are willing to endorse "The Will to Achieve" (W2A), a proposed new national policy model for P-12 education described below.

Step 1: Request public speaking time at a local school board meeting

We start by preparing for the next local school board meeting. We have listed below ten questions you can ask at an agenda item called "Public Speaking Time." Check on local policies, but a common practice is a requirement to sign up for speaking time. Once you get the microphone, you will have only two or three minutes to ask a question. The questions that we suggest will make school board members and school leaders reflect on basic educational premises.

Before these questions, we would like you to familiarize yourself with the first of two powerful ideas introduced by Paulo Freire.

Freire's Limit-Situation

First, Freire described the concept of a "limit-situation"—the absolute dead-end of an endeavor when progress is blocked and no other options appear on the horizon. Yes, American schools have reached such a limit-situation. Do not let your school board members brag about rising scores on district state assessments. The gold standard is the assessment given every other year to a sample of students in Grades 4, 8, and 12 by the National Assessment of Educational Progress (NAEP), "The Nation's Report Card." The bottom line: despite decades of educational reforms and vast expenditures of money, there has been no improvement in student performance since 2006 while many have suffered (Cortez-Rucker et al., 2013).[3]

We will be providing you below with achievement results from 2019 and earlier. Be prepared: you may be asked for more recent results. Calmly respond that in January 2020, the Centers for Disease Control and Prevention (CDC) informed the nation about the Covid-19 outbreak and the 2020–2021 assessments were canceled. Therefore, NAEP tests of 2019 are the baseline because they were administered before the learning disruptions during and after the pandemic. FYI, the post-pandemic scores declined even more precipitously in 2022 with their first administration after the pandemic (Sparks, 2022).[4]

Here are some questions based on NAEP data you should ask your school board members. Mind you, these are questions about national trends, not those of local schools, districts, or states.

Question 1:
Thank you for giving me the opportunity to speak, School Board Members. I would like to discuss trends in reading test scores on the NAEP before the pandemic. When compared to 2017, 2019 scores were lower for both fourth graders and eighth graders in reading (The Nation's Report Card, 2019a).[5] *School board members, we know these are national and not district numbers. But if you had been on the board at that time, would you have worried about those trends?*

Question 2:
To follow up, the average reading score of twelfth graders on the 2019 assessment was 2 points lower than that in 2015 (The Nation's Report Card, 2019b)![6] *If national policies were truly working in the lower grades, shouldn't high school reading scores be improving instead of declining?*

Question 3:
Turning to mathematics, in 2019, average mathematics scores for fourth graders were happily higher than 2017 by 1 point. But they were lower by 1 point for eighth graders. In twelfth grade, the average score math score was not significantly different when compared to 2005 (The Nation's Report Card, 2019c).[7] *Based on this information, would you say our national policies—from which our district policies are drawn—are succeeding?*

Question 4:
Based on 2006–2016 NAEP scores, scholars Michael Petrilli and Eric Hanushek called those years, respectively, "education's lost decade" and "a national embarrassment" (Mahnken, 2018).[8] Timothy Daly, Chief Executive Officer of "EdNavigator," claims we are living through "an education depression." He summarized these conclusions: "2013 turned out to be the high-water mark. Achievement stopped

improving. First, it stagnated. Then, toward the end of 2010s, it began to decline. And finally, along came Covid" (Daly, 2024).[9] *Would you agree with these scholars that something has been seriously wrong with the national education policy which we at our district are mandated to follow?*

Question 5:
Looking at reading scores, Hanushek (2016) noted that after 50+ years of reform, the average black twelfth grader's reading and math scores, when compared to his/her white peers, went from being at the 13th percentile of the score distribution to approximately the 22nd. "If we continue to close gaps at the same rate in the future," he wrote, "it will be roughly 2.5 centuries before the black-white math gap closes and 1.5 centuries until the reading gap closes" (Camera, 2016).[10] *Does the board acknowledge this achievement gap between white and black students? Are board members confident that our policies will fully and quickly eliminate the gap?*

Question 6:
According to the NAEP, the achievement gap between high-performing and low-performing students has grown very significantly (National Assessment Governing Board, 2020).[11] *Should not school reform initiatives be narrowing instead of widening the achievement gap? What is wrong?*

Question 7:
Commenting on test scores right before the pandemic, Beverly Perdue, the chair of the National Assessment Governing Board, stated in 2021: "These results raise the alarm at all levels that education policy to change these results must be a top priority" (Frazier, 2021).[12] *Board members: is this the time to tinker and tweak current policies or must we go back to the drawing board?*

<u>Question 8</u>:
As mentioned above, in the first post-pandemic indicator, reading and math scores for nine-year-olds declined dramatically and gaps by race, academic performance levels, and economic status increased (The Nations Report Card, 2022).[13] *How seriously does the school board recognize this problem?*

Freire's Culture of Silence

Students, we would like you to consider a second important concept of Freire: his notion of the "culture of silence." Paulo Freire had unprecedented success in teaching literacy to very poor farmers working on plantations in Brazil. Most of them had been employed on large plantations called "*latifundium*" where they had no say in their work and developed what he called "a culture of silence." Freire helped peasants analyze their realities and understand the culture of silence imposed on them (Freire, 1984).[14] With this understanding, they were able to quickly learn to read.

The NAEP data described above screams out: "Educational policies are not working for our children." But where is the national outcry from policymakers, academics, the media, or public? Where are the marches? When was educational policy discussed during the 2024 election? (Grose, 2024).[15] We ourselves are suffering from a mass "culture of silence!"

<u>Question 9</u>:
Given the failure of our educational policies indicated by NAEP tests, why is there so little public outcry about failed national policies? *How much discussion is our school board conducting about the failure of national policies?*

<u>Question 10</u>:
Do school board members feel the pain of many students? Many are "voting by their feet" as expressed by chronic student absenteeism. Many teachers are discouraged and express it

by their chronic absenteeism. It seems that our schools have problems staffing both permanent and substitute teachers. Many fewer of us high school students are considering college. Frankly, hardly any of us are considering careers in education. All too often the silence in our classrooms is deafening as teachers have problems conducting stimulating discussions. *Can you join us in promoting dialog about these matters?*

Summary

Thank you very much, students, for opening Freirean dialogs at school board meetings! Through them, you are helping to create an environment that then launches infinitely more dialogs. There are no shortcuts. This slow and difficult work is how we can help break through limit-situations and the culture of silence.

1966: A Short History Lesson

Students, let's hop to some historical background. In 1966 Paulo Freire was living in exile and had turned to organizing poor farmers in Chile. He was most likely at this time drafting ideas for his famous book *Pedagogy of the Oppressed*, which would be published in 1968. What else was happening that year in the United States? The Vietnam War was expanding, Ronald Reagan was elected governor of California, the first Star Trek episode aired, the Beatles played their final concert, and ground was broken for the World Trade Center.

Also in 1966, the *Equality of Educational Opportunity Report* ("the Coleman Report") was surreptitiously released by the Johnson administration (Coleman et al., 1966; Dickenson, 2016; Hill, 2016; Towers, 1992).[16,17,18,19] The findings were so controversial and against the grain that the Johnson administration released the report during the July 4th weekend, hoping to attract minimal public attention (Finn & Lenkowsky, 2020).[20] In one of the largest social science surveys ever conducted, James Coleman and his team concluded that three factors—the conditions of families, neighborhoods, and students' peers—made a far larger impact on children's educational outcomes than any other input—including that of teachers and schools themselves (Dickenson, 2016).[21] Why did the Johnson administration try to silence the report? It's always easier to blame others and keep stirring a boiling kettle than to take direct responsibility for essential matters such as addressing the quality of families, communities, and peers.

Besides some scattered calls for busing and integration, no national dialog followed the release of the report. Few talked honestly about what could be done to work beyond Coleman's harsh conclusions. Where were the discussions about the biggest question: How could every school and student become successful despite all types of histories, inequities, political divisions, and budgetary constraints? This national conversation never happened. The culture of silence in American P-12 education was born.

Policymakers quickly sought to find "exceptions" to Coleman's damning conclusions. Ultimately, they turned to the *"Effective Schools Research Movement"* whose unofficial motto was "All children can learn" (Lezotte, 2001).[22] But it came with a problematic flipside: if some children were not learning, the fault must lie with "failing" teachers, principals, and schools. Policymakers and the media uncritically joined the chorus; blaming a few helpless targets was far easier than the arduous work entailed to jailbreak Coleman's findings.

Blaming teachers and schools had terrible consequences. As the victims were victimized, their voices tapered. Unions began to dig in to protect their members. The "chilling effect" set in (Perrillo, 2024).[23] Teachers became demoralized to the point that we now have teacher shortages. This might have been justifiable if we had seen outstanding academic gains across the board. But, as shown above, such results have not occurred. Instead of liberating the essential energies of teachers and school leaders, especially in schools with underserved populations, we find dysfunctional replicas of *Abbott Elementary* all over the country (Barnum, 2016; Jansen, 1995; Dantley, 1990).[24,25,26]

Step 2: How can we reinvent P-12 education? Start at home!

A note especially to high school students: you are the key to leading Freirean dialogs. There is still time to improve your high school. At the same time, let's take responsibility for improving the schools of your younger brothers and sisters.

Changing American P-12 education is not impossible; it is not even difficult. You and your friends have already broken the ice at many school board meetings. People are now starting to think.

Freire believed that limit-situations should be seen as the entry "where all possibilities begin" (Freire, 2018).[27] The limit-situation in P-12 education is so significant that Freire might insist that people engage in profound and difficult dialogs until ad hoc solutions are forged at multiple levels: homes, schools, districts, states, and at the highest reaches of the national government. But why not start with the people closest to you in your family, school, or community? Shouldn't we start by building a "human" or "life-sized" paradigm for American education (Fullan, 2021; Ikeda, 2003)?[28,29,30,31]

Do not let people box you in! Discussions will be difficult because participants stick to safe proxy cultural and political issues. Do not let discourse go that way! Instead, you must guide the conversation to: "What can we practically do today to help Ms. Janine Teagues' 2nd grade students at Abbott Elementary this Monday morning?"

Try to pose questions like these to parents or significant adults in your life:

- Do you really know the standards for my grade? If not, how can you help me achieve them?

- If parents and guardians taught their children how to read back in the pioneer days, why can't they do the same now?

- Do you think I should come home feeling happy and successful at the end of each school day?

- Do you look forward to Big Stakes Testing Days each year?

- What do you think we can do to close the achievement gap by 2033?

- How can we make it *easy* for students and teachers to *work hard* and achieve brilliantly?

- What would it take to help any student catch up at any time, accelerate learning (and become an electrical engineer)?

- What can we learn and borrow from self-instruction programs like Duolingo, online colleges, homeschooling, Microsoft/Google certifications, etc.?

- How do we rope in all the excellent education content on YouTube and TikTok?

Congratulations, students! You just opened a Freirean dialog with significant adults in your lives and the ripples will spread far and wide. With this under your belt, how about going to the next level?

Step 3: Help find us a champion!

Another note to our high school students: the facts we have discussed so far are harsh and disillusioning. But Freire would tell us today not to despair. Let's think big and follow his example. Can we imagine inviting a massive surge of human resources into our Freirean dialogs? Just envision the active participation of your parents and other adult cheerleaders in your education. Add to that forum teachers-in-the-trenches, community leaders, and students just like you into American P-12 education reform efforts. Do not try to solve everything in a single sweep; instead, open dialog, creativity, collaboration, and experimentation until micro solutions are crafted enabling every child in Ms. Teagues's class to crack the code and break the barriers to unlimited learning.

We are now ready for the third step of activism. Yes, somewhere there is a future candidate for higher office who wants to drive in a lane no one else has traveled before. He or she might see P-12 educational policy as the issue that can excite and unify the country. Don't worry: you already have at hand the campaign speech he or she can use—perhaps in 2028! Find the leader and pass the policy to him or her! Are you ready?

An imagined presidential candidate introduces "The Will To Achieve" (W2A), an imagined new national P-12 educational policy based on Freirean ideas

I am pleased to announce to everyone that I am the first presidential candidate to endorse "The Will to Achieve" (W2A), a proposed new national education policy. Its goal is to smash the ugly achievement gap for students in grades P-8 by 2033, the end of the next president's first administration, and open a new era for our high schools. It will wipe away the exhaustion and frustration about schooling experienced by so many teachers, students, and parents/concerned adults.

W2A recognizes the harsh political realities of the day. During these fractious times, one of the few threads uniting all Americans is our common love for each of our children. So, we must start from the kitchen table and rely on people in the trenches: teachers, parents, and other adults in families, community leaders, and students themselves. For better or worse, due to our political divisions, W2A must be low-cost and depend on the voluntary participation of states.

I believe we must start our work with three premises:

1 Restore the historic partnership of parents and other concerned adult family leaders, teachers, and the community (Brouillette, 1999).[32]

2 Give all parents a clear roadmap to educational success so they know how to help their children.

3 Instill the "Will to Achieve" in the hearts of their children.

The first premise is, in fact, our cultural legacy. We have all read the stories of Laura Ingalls Wilder, who first learned to read from her parents, attended a one-room schoolhouse, and started teaching at the age of fifteen. Other examples abound in our literature and culture as well (Wilder, 1953; Wilder & Williams, 1953; Stuart, 2006; McPhee, 1992).[33,34,35,36,37,38] Nor should we forget the many African American parents and adult caregivers of the Deep South who, in the early twentieth century, built the renowned schools designed by Booker T. Washington and Julius Rosenwald (Deutsch, 2011).[39] The equivalent heroes today are 100 million parents and other adult caregivers who support their children's education and our mighty teachers and principals who are still serving children, swimming against decades of failed federal policies. They are all heroes, and we should never again label them as failures.

The renewal will be accomplished in just four initiatives:

Initiative One: Give parents and other family leaders crystal clear P-8 standards

We need crystal clear standards that every parent and/or family leader can grasp. "Now I know how to help my child!" Let us throw out those "thick" grade-by-grade standards that most family leaders and even many teachers do not understand. Instead, let us talk about standards that family leaders "get"—ones that should be accomplished *at some point* within a "band" of grades, such as early childhood (K-2), upper elementary (3–5), and middle school (6–8). At this crucial time, standards that are "comprehensible" to family leaders are far more important than "comprehensive" ones.

For example, the single standard for English Language Arts in the upper elementary band of grades should be: "*By the end of the upper elementary school grades, my child will be able to read and respond to the great works of children's literature.*" Let families choose the titles of books from a list that reflects their values. That is it: this standard will power a massive family, school, and community effort to read and discuss books

Initiative Two: Open and smart assessments that family heads can support

Every adult family head wants to know how close his or her child is toward achieving the standards—but not at the cost of making the entire school experience revolve around testing! Adult family heads grieve when their children come home with dull and vacant eyes. How will this type of rote schooling produce the brilliant souls who can redirect America in future decades?

At the federal level, we need to end all requirements that mandate states to conduct annual high-stakes assessments for grades 3–8. Instead, we must create assessments that are smart, open, and accurate. For assessments to work they must be a joy to parents and family leaders, something they can understand and support. Let us borrow from the wisdom of our Departments of Motor Vehicles: take the test when the child is ready and try again if he or she fails. A crucial part of open and smart assessments will be home practice tests that are close to 100 percent reliable and valid. There should be absolutely no mysteries; nothing kills the confidence and participation of family heads more than unanticipated surprises.

Students will master a standard at various times and, regardless, let us celebrate whenever one crosses the finish line!

Initiative Three: Mobile 24/7 learning

American students must become the most creative and accomplished in the world. There must be no excuses for failing; it can never be too late to start or to accelerate learning. This requires adopting the vision of the late Clayton Christensen, the scholar of disruptive innovation. Christensen and his colleagues envisioned a national online marketplace—much like a mashed-up Amazon, Google Play/Apple app stores, TeachersPayTeachers, Khan Academy—where mobile "learning apps" can be up/downloaded, rated, and reviewed (Christensen et al., 2010).[40]

Learning apps are designed to teach or review small parts of the curriculum and a key requirement is to make their creation as easy as uploading a TikTok video. Learning apps, free or for pay, can be authored by publishers, teachers, entrepreneurs, students, or family adults. With time, millions of vetted and safe learning apps will appear, each with unique approaches to given topics.

We must aim to open each student's "will to achieve." Students can learn 24/7 on their mobile devices. Instead of being passive consumers of educational content, students take more responsibility for their learning. There will now be more time for athletics, arts, projects, collaboration, reading, research, service, and recreation. The role of teachers will shift; instead of "covering" the curriculum–sometimes for a class of resistant learners—they become coaches and guides to learning.

Initiative Four: School choice on an unprecedented scale

We cannot pretend that what we now have is good enough for our children. In a time of crisis, there is no room for partisanship. Every state needs a fleet of excellent educational programs, whether public, private, parochial, charter, voucher, or homeschooling. Between now and 2033 we need an educational ceasefire, and we must bypass matters of ideology or convention.

We need to develop new forms of the schoolhouse until every child attends a school that enjoys the full support of his or her adult family heads. It must become easy for me to find a school good enough to send my own child!

W2A will provide tools to make it easier to start a new school or "learning community." Teachers are the most undervalued resource in education. They have often been infantilized and have sometimes internalized these attributes; many are exhausted and in despair. We need to start the process whereby teachers can run freely and exhibit their countless gifts. To accomplish this, W2A will provide resources so teacher-powered learning communities can form and thrive in every school and district (Teacher-Powered Schools, n.d.).[41]

Summary

To conclude my speech, the vision for *The Will to Achieve* opens "the will to achieve" in the hearts of our P-8 children. It invites family leaders to be the co-engines of teaching. Communities will be energized to support their families and students. Harsh divisions in our society will be softened and bridged. Our teachers will be seen humming and smiling at the end of every day.

With the implementation of these ideas in grades P-8, the Will to Achieve will bubble up and open the hearts of students as they enter high school. After all, many of my friends in high school were the showrunners of this school reform plan. They conducted thousands of Freirean dialogs at countless school boards and around millions of dining room tables. They are ready to enjoy the fruits of their labors.

But let me say this, however: high school design should be left to individual states or consortia of states. We must align the high school experience to the needs of communities and regional economies. The Department of Education needs a relentless focus on improving P-8 education. If it can't do this, why bother?

One essential discussion remains outstanding: early childhood education. We must invest more in preschool and daycare. We do not want a new level of top-down programs. Instead, we hope to invest in small community-based daycare with associated opportunities for training and nurturing daycare owners, teachers, and parents/family leaders.

As such I say: *The Will to Achieve* will save our schools and save our society. I invite you to join me. Thank you.

Notes

1   Freire, P. (2018). *Pedagogy of the oppressed*. Bloomsbury Academic.

2   Freire, P. (1985). *The politics of education*. Bergin & Garvey.

3   Cortez-Rucker, V., Adams, N., & Cortez-Rucker, S. (2013). Effective schools: A brief review after forty years. *International Journal of Arts and Commerce*, 2(5), 115–22. https://doi.org/10.32804/casirj.

4   Sparks, S. (2022). Two decades of progress, nearly gone: National math, reading scores hit historic lows. *Education Week*. www.edweek.org/leadership/two-decades-of-progress-nearly-gone-national-math-reading-scores-hit-historic-lows/2022/10.

5   The Nation's Report Card (2019a). NAEP Report Card: 2019 NAEP Reading Assessment, Highlighted results at grades 4 and

8 for the nation, states, and district. *NAEP*. Washington, DC: U.S. Department of Education, National Center for Education Statistics. https://www.nationsreportcard.gov/highlights/reading/2019/.

6   The Nation's Report Card (2019b). Lower average reading score for twelfth-graders compared to 2015. *NAEP*. Washington, DC: U.S. Department of Education, National Center for Education Statistics. www.nationsreportcard.gov/reading/nation/scores/?grade=12.

7   The Nation's Report Card (2019c). NAEP Report Card: Mathematics. *NAEP*. Washington, DC: U.S. Department of Education, National Center for Education Statistics. www.nationsreportcard.gov/mathematics/nation/scores/?grade=12https://www.nationsreportcard.gov/highlights/math/2019/.

8   Mahnken, K. (2018). A "Lost Decade" for academic progress? NAEP scores remain flat amid signs of a widening gap between highest and lowest performers. *The 74*. www.the74million.org/article/a-lost-decade-for-academic-progress-naep-scores-remain-flat-amid-signs-of-a-widening-gap-between-highest-and-lowest-performers/.

9   Daly, T. (2024). We're living through an education depression. *The Education Daly*. https://www.educationdaly.us/p/we-are-in-the-midst-of-an-educational.

10   Camera, L. (2016). Achievement gap between white and black students still gaping. *US News*. https://www.usnews.com/news/blogs/data-mine/2016/01/13/achievement-gap-between-white-and-black-students-still-gaping.

11   National Assessment Governing Board (2020). NAEP assessment shows long-term improvement in reading and math, but short-term declines for 13-year-olds. *National Assessment Governing Board*. www.nagb.gov/news-and-events/news-releases/2021/NAEP-Assessment-Shows-Long-Term-Improvement-in-Reading-and-Math.html. "The achievement gap between higher-performing students (those at the 75th and 90th percentiles) and lower-performing students (10th, 25th, and 50th percentiles) has widened significantly since 2012. Whereas there were no significant changes for the higher-performing students, there were significant declines in scores of lower-performing students. This is reflected as well in the

parallel NAEP (not LTT) assessments for 4th and 8th-grade students."

12 Frazier, K. (2021). "Nation's Report Card" finds reading, math test scores falling pre-COVID. *Axios*. October 14. www.axios.com/nations-report-card-falling-reading-math-scores-174a0022-f756-4f31-ad4c-0299bfb20052.html.

13 The Nation's Report Card (2022). 2020 and 2022 long-term trend (LTT) reading and mathematics assessments. *The Nation's Report Card*. https://www.nationsreportcard.gov/highlights/ltt/2022/.

14 Freire, P. (1984). *The politics of education: Culture, power and liberation*. Praeger, p. 22.

15 Grose, J. (2024). The education crisis neither candidate will address. *New York Times*. New York, NY: The New York Times Company. https://www.nytimes.com/2024/10/09/opinion/covid-education-crisis-election.html.

16 Coleman, J. S., United States, & National Center for Education Statistics (1966). *Equality of educational opportunity [summary report]*. Washington, DC: U.S. Department of Health, Education, and Welfare, Office of Education; U.S. Government Printing Office.

17 Dickenson, E. E. (2016). Coleman Report set the standard for the study of public education. *Johns Hopkins Magazine*. Baltimore, MD: Johns Hopkins University. https://hub.jhu.edu/magazine/2016/winter/coleman-report-public-education/.

18 Hill, H. C. (2016). 50 years ago, one report introduced Americans to the black-white achievement gap. Here's what we've learned since. *Chalkbeat*. https://www.chalkbeat.org/2016/7/13/21103280/50-years-ago-one-report-introduced-americans-to-the-black-white-achievement-gap-here-s-what-we-ve-le.

19 Towers, J. M. (1992). Twenty-five Years after the Coleman Report: What should we have learned? *The Clearing House*, 65(3), 138–40. http://www.jstor.org/stable/30188935.

20 Finn, C., & Lenkowsky L. (2020). Inconvenient facts and public policy. *National Affairs*. Washington, DC: National Affairs. https://www.nationalaffairs.com/publications/detail/inconvenient-facts-and-public-policy.

21 Dickenson, E. E. (2016). Coleman Report set the standard for the study of public education. *Johns Hopkins Magazine*. https://hub.jhu.edu/magazine/2016/winter/coleman-report-public-education/.

22 Lezotte, L. (2001). *Revolutionary and evolutionary: The effective schools movement*. Okemos.

23 Perrillo, J. (2024). The chilling effect is real: Educators' stories about preemptive book bans show how schools are censoring themselves. *Slate*. Brooklyn, NY: Slate Group. https://slate.com/life/2024/09/banned-books-week-schools-censorship.html.

24 Barnum, M. (2016). 50 years later, what America still hasn't learned from the Coleman Report. *The 74*. https://www.the74million.org/article/50-years-later-what-america-still-hasnt-learned-from-the-coleman-report/.

25 Jansen, J. D. (1995). Effective schools? *Comparative Education*, *31*(2), 181–200. http://www.jstor.org/stable/3099646.

26 Dantley, M. E. (1990). The ineffectiveness of effective schools leadership: An analysis of the Effective Schools Movement from a critical perspective. *The Journal of Negro Education*, *59*(4), 585–98. https://doi.org/10.2307/2295315.

27 Freire, p. 124.

28 Fullan, M. (2021). *The right drivers for complete system success*. Centre for Strategic Education. https://michaelfullan.ca/wp-content/uploads/2021/03/Fullan-CSE-Leading-Education-Series-01-2021R2-compressed.pdf

29 Fullan, p. 6.

30 Fullan, pp. 8–35.

31 Ikeda, D. (2003). *A global ethic of coexistence: Toward a "life-sized" paradigm for our age*. Soka Gakkai International. www.daisakuikeda.org/main/peacebuild/peace-proposals/pp2003.html.

32 Brouillette, M. J. (1999). *The 1830s and 40s: Horace Mann, the end of free-market education, and the rise of government schools*. Mackinac Center for Public Policy. https://www.mackinac.org/2035.

33 Wilder, L. I. (1953). *Little house in the big woods*. HarperCollins Publishers.

34 Wilder, L. I., & Williams, G. (1953). *On the banks of Plum Creek, revised edition*. HarperCollins.

35 Wilder, L. I., & Jones, C. (2017). *These happy golden years: Little house series, Book 8 (Unabridged)*. HarperCollins.

36 Stuart, J. (2006). *The thread that runs so true*. Jesse Stuart Foundation.

37 McPhee, J. (1992). *The headmaster: Frank L. Boyden of Deerfield*. Farrar, Straus, and Giroux.

38 Stories like Laura Ingalls Wilder include Kentucky poet laureate Jesse Stuart in *The thread that runs so true* began teaching in a rural school at the age of nineteen and quickly rose to principal and superintendent. John McPhee's *The Headmaster* is the story of Frank L. Boyden who became the headmaster of the famed Deerfield Academy at the age of twenty-two and led the school for over sixty-six years.

39 Deutsch, S. (2011). *You need a schoolhouse: Booker T. Washington, Julius Rosenwald, and the building of schools for the segregated South*. Northwestern University Press.

40 Christensen, C. M., Johnson, C. W., Horn, M. H. (2010). *Disrupting class, expanded edition: How disruptive innovation will change the way the world learns 2nd edition, Kindle edition*. McGraw Hill.

41 Teacher-Powered Schools: Student-Centered Learning (n.d.). https://www.teacher-powered.org.

References

Barnum, M. (2016). 50 years later, what America still hasn't learned from the Coleman Report. *The 74*. https://www.the74million.org/article/50-years-later-what-america-still-hasnt-learned-from-the-coleman-report/.

Brouillette, M. J. (1999). *The 1830s and 40s: Horace Mann, the end of free-market education, and the rise of government schools*. Midland, MI: Mackinac Center for Public Policy. https://www.mackinac.org/2035.

Camera, L. (2016). Achievement gap between white and black students still gaping. *US News*. https://www.usnews.com/news/

blogs/data-mine/2016/01/13/achievement-gap-between-white-and-black-students-still-gaping.

Christensen, C. M., Johnson, C. W., & Horn, M. H. (2010). *Disrupting class, expanded edition: How disruptive innovation will change the way the world learns 2nd edition, Kindle edition.* New York, NY: McGraw Hill.

Coleman, J. S., United States, & National Center for Education Statistics (1966). *Equality of educational opportunity [summary report].* Washington, DC: U.S. Dept. of Health, Education, and Welfare, Office of Education; U.S. Government Printing Office.

Cortez-Rucker, V., Adams, N., & Cortez-Rucker, S. (2013). Effective schools: A brief review after forty years. *International Journal of Arts and Commerce,* 2(5), 115–22. https://doi.org/10.32804/casirj.

Daly, T. (2024). We're living through an education depression. *The Education Daly.* https://www.educationdaly.us/p/we-are-in-the-midst-of-an-educational.

Dantley, M. E. (1990). The ineffectiveness of effective schools leadership: An analysis of the Effective Schools Movement from a critical perspective. *The Journal of Negro Education,* 59(4), 585–98. Washington, DC: Howard University (publisher of The Journal of Negro Education). https://doi.org/10.2307/2295315.

Deutsch, S. (2011). *You need a schoolhouse: Booker T. Washington, Julius Rosenwald, and the building of schools for the segregated South.* Ivanston, IL: Northwestern University Press.

Dickenson, E. E. (2016). Coleman Report set the standard for the study of public education. *Johns Hopkins Magazine.* Baltimore, MD: Johns Hopkins University. https://hub.jhu.edu/magazine/2016/winter/coleman-report-public-education/.

Finn, C., & Lenkowsky, L. (2020). Inconvenient facts and public policy. *National Affairs.* Washington, DC: National Affairs. https://www.nationalaffairs.com/publications/detail/inconvenient-facts-and-public-policy.

Frazier, K. (2021). "Nation's Report Card" finds reading, math test scores falling pre-COVID. *Axios.* October 14. Arlington, VA: Axios Media Inc. www.axios.com/nations-report-card-falling-reading-math-scores-174a0022-f756-4f31-ad4c-0299bfb20052.html.

Freire, P. (1984). *The politics of education: Culture, power and liberation.* South Hadley, MA: Bergin & Garvey (Published by Praeger, imprint of Greenwood at the time), p. 22.

Freire, P. (1985). *The politics of education*. Westport, CT: Bergin & Garvey.

Freire, P. (2018). *Pedagogy of the oppressed* (50th Anniversary ed.). New York, NY: Bloomsbury Academic.

Fullan, M. (2021). *The right drivers for whole system success*. East Melbourne: Centre for Strategic Education. https://michaelfullan. ca/wp-content/uploads/2021/03/Fullan-CSE-Leading-Education-Series-01-2021R2-compressed.pdf.

Grose, J. (2024). The education crisis neither candidate will address. *The New York Times*. New York, NY: The New York Times Company. https://www.nytimes.com/2024/10/09/opinion/covid-education-crisis-election.html.

Hanushek, E. A. (2016). What matters for student achievement: Updating Coleman on the influence of families and schools. *Education Next*, 16(2), 22–30. https://www.educationnext.org/what-matters-for-student-achievement/.

Hill, H. C. (2016). 50 years ago, one report introduced Americans to the black-white achievement gap. Here's what we've learned since. New York, NY: Chalkbeat. https://www.chalkbeat. org/2016/7/13/21103280/50-years-ago-one-report-introduced-americans-to-the-black-white-achievement-gap-here-s-what-we-ve-le.

Ikeda, D. (2003). *A global ethic of coexistence: Toward a "life-sized" paradigm for our age*. Tokyo: Soka Gakkai International. www. daisakuikeda.org/main/peacebuild/peace-proposals/pp2003.html.

Jansen, J. D. (1995). Effective schools? *Comparative Education*, 31(2), 181–200. Abingdon: Taylor & Francis (publisher of Comparative Education). http://www.jstor.org/stable/3099646.

Lezotte, L. (2001). *Revolutionary and evolutionary: The effective schools movement*. Okemos, MI: Okemos.

Mahnken, K. (2018). A "Lost Decade" for academic progress? NAEP scores remain flat amid signs of a widening gap between highest and lowest performers. *The 74*. www.the74million.org/article/a-lost-decade-for-academic-progress-naep-scores-remain-flat-amid-signs-of-a-widening-gap-between-highest-and-lowest-performers/.

McPhee, J. (1992). *The headmaster: Frank L. Boyden of Deerfield*. New York, NY: Farrar, Straus, and Giroux.

National Assessment Governing Board (2020). NAEP assessment shows long-term improvement in reading and math, but short-term declines for 13-year-olds. *National Assessment Governing Board*. Washington, DC: U.S. Department of Education. www.nagb.gov/news-and-events/news-releases/2021/NAEP-Assessment-Shows-Long-Term-Improvement-in-Reading-and-Math.html. "The achievement gap between higher-performing students (those at the 75th and 90th percentiles) and lower-performing students (10th, 25th, and 50th percentiles) has widened significantly since 2012. Whereas there were no significant changes for the higher-performing students, there were significant declines in scores of lower-performing students. This is reflected as well in the parallel NAEP (not LTT) assessments for 4th and 8th-grade students."

Perrillo, J. (2024). The chilling effect is real: Educators' stories about preemptive book bans show how schools are censoring themselves. *Slate*. Brooklyn, NY: Slate Group. https://slate.com/life/2024/09/banned-books-week-schools-censorship.html.

Sparks, S. (2022). Two decades of progress, nearly gone: National math, reading scores hit historic lows. *Education Week*. Bethesda, MD: Editorial Projects in Education, Inc. www.edweek.org/leadership/two-decades-of-progress-nearly-gone-national-math-reading-scores-hit-historic-lows/2022/10.

Stuart, J. (2006). *The thread that runs so true*. Ashland, KY: Jesse Stuart Foundation.

Teacher-Powered Schools: Student-Centered Learning (n.d.). https://www.teacher-powered.org

The Nation's Report Card (2019a). NAEP Report Card: 2019 NAEP Reading Assessment, Highlighted results at grades 4 and 8 for the nation, states, and district. *NAEP*. Washington, DC: U.S. Department of Education, National Center for Education Statistics. https://www.nationsreportcard.gov/highlights/reading/2019/.

The Nation's Report Card (2019b). Lower average reading score for twelfth-graders compared to 2015. *NAEP*. Washington, DC: U.S. Department of Education, National Center for Education Statistics. www.nationsreportcard.gov/reading/nation/scores/?grade=12.

The Nation's Report Card (2019c). NAEP Report Card: Mathematics. *NAEP*. Washington, DC: U.S. Department of Education, National Center for Education Statistics. www.nationsreportcard.gov/mathematics/nation/scores/?grade=12https://www.nationsreportcard.gov/highlights/math/2019/.

The Nation's Report Card (2022). 2020 and 2022 long-term trend (LTT) reading and mathematics assessments. *The Nation's Report Card*. Washington, DC: U.S. Department of Education, National Center for Education Statistics. https://www.nationsreportcard.gov/highlights/ltt/2022/.

Towers, J. M. (1992). Twenty-five years after the Coleman Report: What should we have learned? *The Clearing House*, 65(3), 138–40. Washington, DC: Taylor & Francis (current publisher of The Clearing House). http://www.jstor.org/stable/30188935.

Wilder, L. I. (1953). *Little house in the big woods*. New York, NY: Harper & Brothers.

Wilder, L. I., & Jones, C. (2017). *These happy golden years: Little house series, Book 8 (Unabridged)*. New York, NY: HarperCollins.

Wilder, L. I., & Williams, G. (1953). *On the banks of Plum Creek*, (revised ed.). New York, NY: Harper & Brothers.

CHAPTER FIVE

Ecopedagogy in the Elementary School Classroom

Michaela L. Ensweiler

Background

Ecopedagogy is an environmental pedagogy rooted in popular education pedagogies, theories, and philosophies—they have grounding in Freirean models of democratically structured critical study, cooperative dialogic, and action. The specific goal of ecopedagogy is to critically examine connections between human acts of environmental ills (the world) and how these affect Nature, making up Earth. Ecopedagogy centers Earth as among the oppressed (Misiaszek & Torres, 2019). Education, then, must expand anthropological and anthropocentric reflections to include Nature and Earth in order to end oppression—to quote Robin Wall Kimmerer "What we do to the land we do to ourselves" (2013, p. 258). Education in this regard must have the goal of transformational praxis—it is not theory in itself or abstract but continuous reading and reflections to guide our practices.

Ecopedagogy also calls us to deepen and widen our reflections (Misiaszek, 2018) in a local–global–local dialect that is always in conversation. We must reach deeply into our local environment to problematize acts of oppression. When we've identified systems that are unsustainable and have problematized them, we can widen our problematization to uncover systems of oppression in the global. When we've actively problematized and reflected on these oppressions, we can then act in the form of praxis in our local to attempt to create systemic change on a local–global–local scale. This process is not always a linear progression as local praxis can also be global praxis and vice versa, this is a holistic process of examination and change. The local is dependent on global influences as is the global dependent on local influence, thus only understood in relation with each other as one is constantly affecting the other.

My lens of ecopedagogical praxis is food—foodways, food systems, and what I refer to as the Food–Culture Divide. Food can enter a classroom in many ways and can be examined in an ecopedagogical manner. This lesson plan will mimic a well-known scientific experiment in an elementary classroom with specific moves to deepen and widen students'[1] perspectives to garner ecopedagogical awareness and foment greater relationships with Nature and Earth as it relates to food. The experiment is a well-known activity that can allow a teacher to transgress (hooks, 1994) in that it breeds excitement, curiosity, and a dialogic collaboration that is liberating from "banking education" and unsustainable oppressions.

The experiment being utilized in this chapter is a biology experiment that can be found here: https://www.pbs.org/parents/crafts-and-experiments/rainbow-celery-experiment

The structure of this chapter's lesson is mimicking the steps in a 5E model (Bybee, 2009), that has been used in my classrooms previously. The steps in this model are as follows: engage, explore, explain, elaborate, and evaluate. This chapter's lesson plan integrates Freirean aspects to the 5E model in order to extend dialog from a student's local positionality to a global lens of sustainability issues.

Supplies	Set-up
For this experiment, you will need a plant or a food that quickly soaks in water so that you would be able to see if the water had food coloring applied. For our classroom, we utilized celery. You will need containers for one or two different colors of water as well as food coloring to color the water a different color.	I like to fill multiple containers with different colors of water and set celery to the side before revealing the experiment to introduce the class to the activity. This works best in pairs or groups with roles for students to interact with. There can be a scribe in the pair or group, for example, as well as a group member to collect the items, a group member to record time, etc. This encourages the Freirean aspect of dialog, collective meaning-making, and collaboration for students. Students can record their thoughts in a journal, on a piece of paper, a poster, or a computer in words or pictures.

What We Know (Local Knowledge/ Readings)

In a whole group setting, while introducing the activity, ask your students what they see on the table. What do they know about water? What do they know about food coloring and how it acts when it's placed in water? What do they know about celery? Where does celery come from? What kinds of things does celery need to survive? How does celery relate to us?

This act is dialogically reading the world to read the word—examining local and personal knowledges as it relates to what is seen on the table. Collaborative and collective meaning-making and (re)naming can take place during this stage as our community of learners are able to utilize differing perspectives and ways of knowing—epistemological pluralism.

Start to explain what the process of the experiment will be—we will be coloring the water with food dye and placing celery in the water.

Predictions (Problematization)

After explaining the process and showing how to dye the water and place the celery in it (or in multiple cups), ask the students about their predictions: what do you think might happen? Will something change in the water? Will something change in the celery? Might something even happen to us?

Again, utilize the collaborative and collective meaning-making in this scenario. This is an example of problematization—students can see the concept but have the ability to ask questions about the objects and actions together. Furthermore, when a collective prediction has been made, problematize it further with more objects and actions. This is widening their understanding, and we will return to this idea after the experiment has concluded.

Observation (Reading)

Now it is time for the community of learners to try the experiment for themselves, observe what happens, and draw conclusions to prepare for reflections and extensions.

Let the learners explore the task in groups, pairs, or individually. If learners are in groups, assigning roles to the group members may aid in the facilitation of the experiment. A learner may be a timekeeper, item collector, recorder, or sketch artist. Time the experiment, ensure the learners are observing any changes and marking times of said changes. Let learners read the world in this instance: what is happening? Is anything changing? Why is it or is it not changing?

Learners collaboratively or independently are reading their world to read the word (Freire, 1983). They must (re)name, contextualize, and explain what is happening in order to form praxis around a given situation. This is a local understanding and will be challenged in a wider global understanding after they've successfully read their world.

Reflections and Extensions

After the experiment has concluded, allow learners back as a whole-group community to reflect on their readings (observations). What happened? Why did this happen? Extend their reading from local understanding (what happened in their reading) to a global understanding in "What might happen if" scenarios. What might happen if something else were placed in the water? What might happen if something else was in the water?

An idea for an upper-elementary class is extending this to the study of water and agriculture. There are many instances where water can become contaminated—what might that do to the plants and animals that depend on it? Moreover, agriculture can also contaminate water—what consequences might that have?

This extension can widen learners' understanding to a global lens as well by challenging their understanding of waterways and foodways. Could a contaminant in a waterway elsewhere affect a waterway locally? Could a contaminated field locally affect a waterway or field elsewhere?

For an idea on an article, see: https://news.mongabay.com/2022/09/humans-are-dosing-earths-waterways-with-medicines-it-isnt-healthy/ The 2020 global Covid-19 pandemic had many effects on a local–global–local scale. This is one instance where waterways were affected by a medicine used during the pandemic. Might this have an effect on where we live? Then or now? Could it influence somewhere else?

Action

When the extension conversations have concluded, dialog through this praxis as praxis is embodied through these various interactions. It is in praxis that meanings are created, and this is an opportunity to collaborate on the differing stories, thoughts, and perspectives of our learners. Learners have taken a path of problematization, reading the world, reflecting, and extending their knowledge. Think about your local fields, foodways, and waterways. Problematize one—is there a local waterway that has been polluted? Is there a local foodway that is a contaminant? Is there a local field that might affect a waterway?

Extend the experiment to praxis by visiting these local sites, problematizing, reading, and reflecting. Deepen and widen understandings by seeking out their histories locally and understanding their global impacts. Take action by reaching out to local authorities, cleaning a polluted location, or notifying the public.

Drawings/Sketches

Remember to add multiple modes of accessibility to the reading of this experiment—learners may use this space to draw what they see. Perhaps they can draw a comic like the one pictured here:

Notes

Some learners may be more inclined to write or research while enacting this lesson. Make this lesson available on paper or utilize technology by having students create a PowerPoint, TikTok, or other forms of media.

This lesson can and should be modified to suit specific learning spaces in differing locales with different scaffolds that engage multiple modes of inquiry and engagement. It is my hope that this lesson can be utilized as a spark, an idea, a dialog through which learners, educational spaces, and educators are able to explore acts of oppression with human and non-human entities in order to create agents of hope, love, and change for current and future entities.

Conclusions

Ecopedagogy can offer learners a transformative approach to education that emphasizes relationships and interconnections of humans and Earth through human actions and environmental health. Ecopedagogy asks us "Who benefits, who pays, and who suffers" (Misiaszek, 2018) in these actions in local and global spheres. While learners explore through embodied experiences, they integrate local perspectives and understandings to familiarize globalized and Earthly issues. This allows learners to step into these varying and multifaceted issues while also asking questions of who benefits, who pays, and who suffers. By integrating these ecopedagogical principles into formal elementary education curricula, educators can foster a deeper and wider understanding of environmental and world-Earth issues to inspire learners to become active agents in creating a more just and sustainable citizenry. This approach not only enhances learners' academic knowledge but also cultivates a sense of connection and community, responsibility and reciprocity with Earth, with all of Earth's beings and systems, as well as with each other.

This experiment serves as a practical example and gateway of how ecopedagogy could be explored in a formal elementary school classroom. Through this activity, learners engaged through embodied experiences; learned how to observe, predict, and reflect on outcomes that connect their experiences to broader global issues; and encouraged them to explore. This process of local–global–local dialect helps learners understand the impact of human actions on environments and encourages them to think critically about sustainable praxis.

Praxis, action reoccurring throughout the learning process, can be reflective and transformative. The process is ever-coalescing in learning spaces. This lesson can lead to more noticing or wondering that can be explored through similar means, making the connection and relationship between learners and Earth even stronger.

Note

1   The words "student" and "learner" will be utilized interchangeably within this chapter as we are all interchangeably both at any given time.

References

Bybee, R. W. (2009). The BSCS 5E instructional model and 21st century Skills. A commissioned paper prepared for a workshop on exploring the intersection of science education and the development of 21st century skills.Available www.bscs.org. [Accessed May 9, 2017].

Freire, P. (1983). The importance of the act of reading. *Journal of Education*, 165(1), 5–11. https://doi. org/10.1177/002205748316500103.

Harris, M. (2020). Celery food coloring experiment. PBS KIDS for Parents. January 2. https://www.pbs.org/parents/crafts-and-experiments/rainbow-celery-experiment.

hooks, b. (1994). *Teaching to transgress: Education as the practice of freedom*. London: Routledge.

Kimmerer, R. (2013). *Braiding sweetgrass: Indigenous wisdom, scientific knowledge and the teachings of plants*. Minneapolis, MN: Milkweed Editions.

Misiaszek, G. W. (2018). *Educating the global environmental citizen: Understanding ecopedagogy in local and global contexts*. London and New York, NY: Routledge.

Misiaszek, G. W., & Torres, C. A. (2019). Ecopedagogy: The missing chapter of Pedagogy of the Oppressed. In C. A. Torres (Ed.), *The Wiley handbook of Paulo Freire* (pp. 463–88). Hoboken, NJ: John Wiley & Sons.

Scherer, G. (2022). Humans are dosing Earth's waterways with medicines. It isn't healthy. *Mongabay Environmental News*. September 22. https://news.mongabay.com/2022/09/humans-are-dosing-earths-waterways-with-medicines-it-isnt-healthy/.

CHAPTER SIX

Critical Pedagogy of Counter-Storytelling in Fifth-Grade Classrooms: Witnessing Stories of Students and Families

Moraima Machado

US schools—either by design or unwittingly—often neglect to embrace the increased cultural and linguistic diversity and strengths that People of Color bring to the society and thus contribute to oppression of students. Because school systems rely on a Eurocentric curricula that erase the stories of Youth of Color, use pedagogical approaches that elevate the dominant culture, and devalue indigenous epistemology (Delgado Bernal, 2002; Gay, 2018; Khalifa, 2018; Ladson-Billings, 2009; Mills, 1997), schools maintain the dominant narrative and silence Communities of Color. Thus, centering the voices and histories of Students of Color[1] in our classrooms is a revolutionary act vital to supporting Students of Color to be academically successful (Cruz, 2016; Delgado, 1989; Delgado Bernal et al., 2016; Machado, 2021; Solórzano & Yosso, 2002).

In this study, I partnered with teachers, families, and a community member to honor the stories of families and students as hallmarks of critical literacy possibilities (Muhammad, 2018). The participatory activist action research (PAAR) project and study took place in an elementary school in a medium-sized urban district in Northern California. To the traditional action research process of engaging participants and myself as observers participating in cycles of inquiry (Bryk et al., 2015; Herr & Anderson, 2014), I added activist participatory action research in which the researchers are dedicated to changing the way people work as social justice advocates. We investigated how the curriculum could be more responsive to the lived experiences of students and families in the school community. By utilizing Community Learning Exchanges (CLEs) axioms and processes (Guajardo et al., 2016), we placed the assets of our racially diverse population—rich experiences, histories, and cultures—front and center. Our purpose was to counteract the dominant narrative of Students of Color as deficient, "less than," or *"pobrecitos"* who are often characterized as unable to succeed.

1. Learning and Leadership are dynamic social processes.

2. Conversations are critical and central pedagogical processes.

3. The people closest to the issues are best situated to discover answers to local concerns.

4. Crossing boundaries enriches development and the educational processes.

5. Hope and change are built on assets and dreams of local and their communities.

We engaged in three cycles of inquiry in which we used iterative, qualitative evidence to understand how to best engage with students and families. In the first cycle of inquiry at a CLE, we focused on bringing families together to understand the power of their stories and then meeting to tell our stories. In the second cycle of inquiry, the team engaged in reflective dialog to co-analyze the learning from the family stories and then used the stories to design the storytelling curriculum for the fifth-grade students. In the third inquiry cycle, teachers implemented the storytelling curriculum in the fifth grade. Students interviewed their parents and grandparents to write "I Come From" poems, narratives of their stories. Families joined students when they presented their poems, building a sense of community pride as the children shared their ancestral knowledge.

Stories of Practice and Reflection

A key factor in the PAAR project and study was the emphasis on combining critical pedagogy, dialogic practice (Freire, 1970; Hale, 2008; Hale, 2017; Hunter et al., 2013) and the CLEs axioms. Through our collective work, teachers and school administrators needed to be willing to engage in authentic dialog with families, to redefine the roles of teachers and school leaders in school, and to engage in a different kind of listening—listening as a witness.

Freire's Authentic Dialog

Freire (1970) emphasized that dialog requires both reflection and action. When people engage in authentic dialog, they reflect not simply internally but to influence change. Rather than the traditional hierarchical approach in which information is presented to teachers, students, and parents using a banking model of depositing, we employed a Freirean approach to our collaborative work. Our work required engaging in authentic dialog and redefining the roles of teachers and leaders in school. Authentic dialog required holding the space, attending to the relationships, legitimizing new knowledge from Communities of Color, and witnessing—not simply listening—to each other's stories. Teachers held space by ensuring that everyone contributed and acknowledging how their students added new knowledge by sharing their cultural wealth.

In classrooms, authentic dialog occurred when teachers created the "container," a safe space, for students to share their stories. Holding space has these features: "recognizing and confirming the person … pushing appropriately to ask the person to challenge or stretch … and [be a place] where a person can grow into new ways of knowing" (Drago-Severson, 2012, p. 47). These factors are as important for adult learning as they are for students. By asking two reflective questions— how sharing your story made you feel and how listening to the story shared by your classmates made you feel—the teachers held the space by confirming each student and gradually pushing them to be more vulnerable. Authentic dialog occurred when students were not competing for or debating their ideas but rather seeking to understand each other's stories.

Authentic dialog and storytelling were complementary in that they offered us processes in which we could draw from our funds of knowledge to collaborate in centering the voices of Students of Color in the school (Moll et al., 1992). Thus, we fostered a shift from hierarchical to horizontal relationships.

Changing Power Relationships from Hierarchical to Horizontal

Freire (1970) states that dialog requires horizontal relationships "which lead the dialoguers into ever closer partnership" (p. 91). The process of storytelling required redefining roles from hierarchical to horizontal relationships among participants. The power relationship shifted as teachers and students were teachers and learners of each other's stories. When implementing the storytelling curriculum, teachers attended to relationships and gradually shifted their role to that of holding the space for listening and witnessing counterstories. As students experienced vulnerability in their classrooms and shared their family stories, a sense of community emerged (Delgado Bernal et al., 2016; Guajardo & Guajardo, 2013; Prieto & Villenas, 2016).

Holding the space in classrooms for storytelling required teachers to shift from soliciting stories as an assignment to listening and witnessing counterstories (see Figure 6.1). Witnessing a story is more than just listening or hearing, Instead the listeners are first in a position of self-reflection and move toward empathetic responses as they "travel" to another's world. Witnessing a story means listening with nonjudgment, listening with love, listening to be fully present and to be vulnerable (Cruz, 2016).

A notable change occurred in the third cycle of the PAAR study regarding how teachers encouraged stories from the students. In the second cycle of the PAAR project, we reflected on how storytelling was not an assignment to complete; instead, storytelling was the process in which we committed

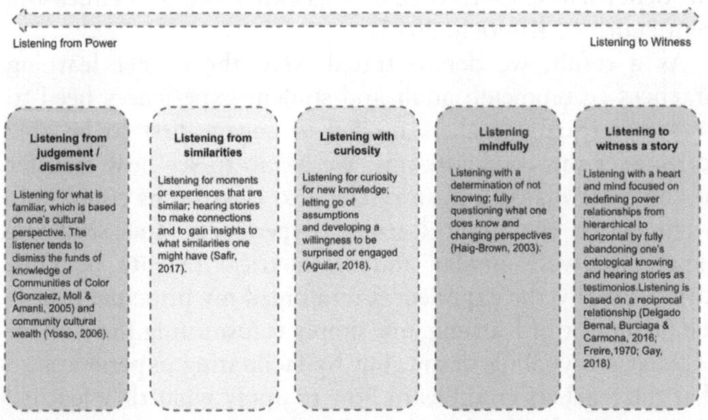

FIGURE 6.1 *Storytelling through testimonios: The path to witnessing.*

ourselves to listen and learn. As Shor and Freire (1987) state, "dialogue is a way to recreate knowledge as well as the way to learn it" (p. 11). Through reflections and conversations with teachers and in meetings, we observed that teachers began to shift their practices because of these new ways of doing and knowing. In previous years, they asked students to write stories about themselves as an assignment to be graded. As a result of shifts in their engagement, teachers listened to and witnessed the stories with the end goal of sustaining a community of student learners. Teachers redefined their roles as the holders of knowledge and located themselves in the role of learners in their classrooms.

Parallel Process

Experiential learning (Dewey, 1938) is essential for teachers if we expect them to facilitate authentic dialog and storytelling in their classrooms. As I engaged all teachers in sharing stories and centering our daily experiences at meetings to learn from each other, we developed relationships and experienced not only the value of listening but being witnesses to each other's experiences as educators (San Pedro & Kinloch, 2017).

As a result, we demonstrated what the deeper learning practices recommend: adult and student experiences need to be symmetrical—teachers needed to engage first to be able to transfer this to classrooms. We began to see how transfer of authentic dialog and storytelling to classrooms could only occur when the adult learning experiences and students' experience were similar and symmetrical (Mehta & Fine, 2015). Finally, the experiences reinforced my principal role as the facilitator of learning, not simply transmitting the content of what storytelling meant, but by facilitating experiences so that the teachers could learn how to apply what they learned about storytelling with their students. Participants shifted their practices to their classrooms because they experienced the practice in our meetings.

From Listening to Witnessing Stories

Modeling vulnerability was an important practice for teachers to begin listening as witnesses of the stories. In the first cycle of inquiry, parents, community members, and I first modeled vulnerability by sharing counterstories. Then, in the second cycle of inquiry, the teachers became gradually more vulnerable with their students in their classrooms. For example, Jessica, a fifth-grade teacher and CPR group member, shared her reflections,

> As I listened to the parents so excited to share their stories and so excited to share their little window into their world, and I thought, how cool is that? But then at the same time, I was like, wow, there's so much that I haven't shared with my kids about me. That I certainly could, and I feel that they would know me better and appreciate me better as their teacher.

This reveals how the teacher's recognition of the importance of her vulnerability with students increased by listening to the parents being vulnerable. As teachers experienced listening to witness, they began to see their experiences and the power of story as a moving force for change (Dewey, 1938). As they transferred the knowledge of how to maintain the space for sharing stories, they attended to relationships differently, honored and valued stories in their classrooms, and became fully witnesses.

A Collective Story of Change in Action

Learning to witness stories is a pedagogical practice that centers the voices of Students of Color in classrooms. As teachers developed dialogical relationships with students and situated their relationships in "the culture, language, politics, and themes of the students" (Shor & Freire, 1987,

p. 18), they shifted their roles in the classroom. The horizontal dialog between teachers and students becomes a natural part of the process of knowing (Freire, 1985). In examining our participatory action and activist research, we learned that to engage in authentic dialog school leaders needed to be vulnerable to share their stories and be willing to "break down the walls" that separate teachers from the communities they serve (Freire, 1970; Freire, 1985; Howard, 2016; Gay, 2018). For this change to occur, teachers and student experiences needed to be symmetrical, meaning that teachers needed to be in a space that supports them to be learners of their stories first, before they can implement storytelling in their classrooms. Because we created the conditions to learn, teachers positioned themselves as teachers and learners in their classrooms (Freire, 1985).

This activist approach adds to the literature of Freire's views of dialogical methodology of investigation and generative themes (Freire, 1970). We attended to generative themes that emerged from the work to co-create the storytelling curriculum. In the process of designing and implementing the curriculum, we learned that the research process is one of "witnessing." By centering the stories of Students and Families of Color, teachers and community members, we created the conditions—the space—for participants to engage in horizontal relationships. In doing so, we gradually moved from listening from a position of power—using our authority/experiences as the norm to judge stories—to listening as "witnesses"—acknowledging and centering the funds of knowledge and cultural wealth of People of Color (Yosso, 2006).

In the process, we became researchers of our lived experiences and connected to our individual and collective larger experience as immigrants, parents, and professionals. These stories were more than just stories shared; they were *testimonios*, a stronger word in Spanish that means a public statement that points to issues of resistance and oppression. "In listening to the story of one, we learned about the conditions of many" (Delgado Bernal et al., 2016). The research was not a process of extracting information from students, families, and teachers but a process of listening for the forces of hope, love, dreams, as well as struggles and pain that we can use to a larger focus of storytelling as a critical literacy (Freire, 1970; Freire, 1985; MacDonald, 1996).

Education as a process of witnessing rather than merely hearing is a revolutionary concept. This is the political act of education that Freire (1985) names, which requires educators and school leaders to engage in a process of reflection and action guided by strong feelings of love for students and communities. To truly witness the stories of Communities of Color, educators need to be willing to engage in the process of critical consciousness—*conscientização*—unmask privilege and recognize that their power is the oppression of others. To be a witness, an educator would need to share with students their story as an oppressor. Then, and only then, would a community begin to heal from the wounds that systemic oppression has created and to see each other as fellows where the stories become the foundation of our communities.

Note

1   Throughout the article, following Pérez-Huber and Cueva (2012) rationale, I use the terms "People of Color," "Students of Color," "Communities of Color," and "Families of Color"; the intentional use of capital letters offers "a means of empowerment and represents a grammatical move toward social justice" (p. 406).

References

Bryk, A. S., Gomez, L. M., Grunow, A., & LaMahieu, P. G. (2015). *Learning to improve: How America's schools can get better at getting better*. Cambridge, MA: Harvard Education Press.

Cruz, C. (2016). Making curriculum from scratch: Testimonio in an urban classroom. In D. Delgado Bernal, R. Burciaga, & J. Flores Carmona (Eds.), *Chicana/Latina testimonios as pedagogical, methodological, and activist approaches to social justice* (pp. 97–108). New York, NY: Routledge.

Delgado, R. (1989). Storytelling for oppositionists and others: A plea for narrative. *Michigan Law Review*, 87(8), 2411–41. Ann Arbor, MI: University of Michigan Law School.

Delgado Bernal, D. (2002). Critical race theory, Latino critical theory, and critical race gendered epistemologies: Recognizing students of color as holders and creators of knowledge. *Qualitative Inquiry*, 8(1), 105–26. Thousand Oaks, CA: Sage Publications.

Delgado Bernal, D., Burciaga, R., & Flores Carmona, J. (2016). Chicana/ Latina testimonios: Mapping the methodological, pedagogical and political. In D. Delgado Bernal, R. Burciaga, & J. Flores Carmona (Eds.), *Chicana/Latina testimonios as pedagogical, methodological, and activist approaches to social justice* (pp. 1–10). New York, NY: Routledge.

Dewey, J. (1938). *Experience & education*. New York, NY: Touchstone / Simon & Schuster.

Drago-Severson, E. (2012). *Helping educators grow: Strategies and practices for leadership development*. Cambridge, MA: Harvard Education Press.

Freire, P. (1970). *Pedagogy of the oppressed*. New York, NY: Bloomsbury Publishing Inc.

Freire, P. (1985). Reading the world and reading the word: An interview with Paulo Freire. *Language Art*, 62(1), 15–21. Urbana, IL: National Council of Teachers of English (NCTE).

Gay, G. (2018). *Culturally responsive teaching: Theory, research, and practice* (3rd ed.). New York, NY: Teachers College Press.

Guajardo, F., & Guajardo, M. (2013). The power of plática. *Reflections: A Journal of Public Rhetoric, Civic Writing, and Service*, 13(1), 159–64.

Guajardo, M., Guajardo, F., Janson, C., & Militello, M. (2016). *Reframing community partnerships in education: Uniting the power of place and wisdom of people*. New York, NY: Routledge.

Gutiérrez, K. D. (2016). Developing a sociocritical literacy in the third space. *Reading Research Quarterly*, 43(2), 148–64. Newark, DE: International Literacy Association.

Hale, C. R. (2008). *Engaging contradictions: Theory, politics, and methods of activist scholarship*. Berkeley, CA: University of California Press.

Hale, C. R. (2017). What is activist research? *Items and Issues, 2*(1), 13–19. New York, NY: Social Science Research Center.

Herr, K., & Anderson, G. (2014). *The action research dissertation: A guide for students and faculty* (2nd ed.). Thousand Oaks, CA: Sage.

Howard, G. R. (2016). We Can't Teach What We Don't Know: White teachers, multiracial schools, third edition . Teachers College Press.

Hunter, L., Emerald, E., & Martin, G. (2013). *Participatory activist research in the globalized world*. Dordrecht: Springer.

Jimenez, R. (2010). Education and empowerment: Critical pedagogy, community wealth and family histories with a sixth-grade teacher and her Mexican immigrant students (Order No. 3452023) [Doctoral Dissertation, U.C. Los Angeles]. ProQuest Dissertations and Theses Global.

Khalifa, M. (2018). *Culturally responsive school leadership*. Cambridge, MA: Harvard Education Press.

Ladson-Billings, G. (2009). *The dreamkeepers: Successful teachers of African American children* (2nd ed.). San Francisco, CA: Jossey-Bass Publishers.

MacDonald, J. P. (1996). *Redesigning schools: Lessons for the 21st century*. San Francisco, CA: Jossey-Bass.

Machado, M. (2021). Family Stories Matter: Critical Pedagogy of Storytelling in Fifth-Grade Classrooms [Doctoral Dissertation, East Carolina University]. May. Greenville, NC: East Carolina University. Retrieved from the Scholarship. http://hdl.handle.net/10342/9084.

Mehta, J., & Fine, S. (2015). *The why, what, where, and how of deeper learning in American secondary schools*. Boston, MA: Jobs for the Future. https://www.jff.org/resources/why-what-where-and-how-deeper-learning-american-secondary-schools/.

Mills, C. (1997). *The racial contract*. Ithaca, NY: Cornell University.

Moll, L., Amanti, C., Neff, D., & Gonzalez, N. (1992). Funds of knowledge for teaching: Using a qualitative approach to connect homes and classrooms. *Theory into Practice, 31*(2), 131–41. Washington, DC: Taylor & Francis.

Muhammad, G. E. (2018) A plea for identity and criticality: Reframing literacy learning standards through a four-layered equity model. *Journal of Adolescent & Adult Literacy*, 62(2), 137–42. Newark, DE: International Literacy Association.

Pérez Huber, L., & Cueva, M. B. (2012). Chicana/Latina testimonios on effects and responses to microaggressions. *Equity & Excellence in Education*, 45(3), 392–410. Abingdon: Routledge.

Prieto, L., & Villenas, S. A. (2016). Pedagogies from neplanta: Testimonio, Chicana/Latina feminisms and teacher education classrooms. In D. Delgado Bernal, R. Burciaga, & J. Flores Carmona (Eds.), *Chicana/Latina testimonios as pedagogical, methodological, and activist approaches to social justice* (pp. 97–108). New York, NY: Routledge.

San Pedro, T., & Kinloch, V. (2017). Towards projects in humanization: Research on co-creating and sustaining dialogic relationships. *American Educational Research Journal*, 54(15), 373S–394S. Washington, DC: American Educational Research Association.

Shor, I., & Freire, P. (1987). What is the "dialogical method" of teaching? *Journal of Education*, 169(3), 11–31. Boston, MA: Boston University School of Education.

Solórzano, D. G., & Yosso, T. J. (2002). Critical race methodology: Counter-storytelling as an analytical framework for educational research. *Qualitative Inquiry*, 8(1), 23–44. Thousand Oaks, CA: Sage Publications.

Yosso, T. J. (2006). *Critical race counterstories along the Chicana/Chicano educational pipeline*. New York, NY: Routledge.

CHAPTER SEVEN

Global Citizenship, Women, and Leadership: Through the Lens of Critical Pedagogy

Maria Guajardo

> *Discrimination against women, expressed and committed by sexist discourse … is incompatible with any progressive position … The rejection of a sexist ideology … involves the re-creation of language, [and] is part of the possible dream of a change of the world.*
>
> (FREIRE, 1994, p. 67)

Imagining a changed world is what brought me to teaching. Engaging with students, I discovered the challenge and magic of teaching, working intentionally to create a transformational learning experience. As a professor in the field of leadership studies, I was trained and educated in the United States, the Global North, from a Western leadership perspective. While preparing to teach leadership courses to a diverse range of students in Tokyo, Japan, I discovered leadership textbooks were typically written by white men from the Global North, rarely identifying their positionality as Western and male-centric. I questioned the relevance of the texts given the absence of representation of diverse voices. The male-based perspective of leadership was normalized, while the inclusion of female perspectives or views from marginalized communities was usually an add-on chapter at the end of the textbook (e.g., Northhouse, 2017). As I broadened my worldview of leadership through the inclusion of diverse scholars, diverse student voices, and my own experiences, my understanding of leadership radically transformed. Leadership for social change and as a process of transformation became central to my definition of leadership. At its core was a question of purpose and power: leadership for what purpose and whose voice is included, excluded, and/ or silenced. This focus on purpose and power mirrored my approach to global citizenship education (GCE), which is inextricably linked to leadership.

Global Citizenship Education

"Global Citizenship Education (GCE)" is a problem-posing education examining social justice and sustainability in all communities. This is in line with Torres and Bosio's (2020) view that GCE is a process rather than a static curriculum.

This chapter examines how the principles of practice in critical pedagogy (CP) (Freire, 1970) can impact global citizenship and leadership to become more inclusive. CP is a practice of engagement through dialog and critical inquiry, questioning how power works and how to use power in the service of justice. The hope is that current and future educators will be encouraged to apply Freirean concepts in their teaching, reimagining the classroom as a space for building community and a sense of belonging.

The challenge of the twenty-First century is to shift toward a social justice perspective inclusive of diverse voices, including women's voices. Believing that a gendered approach to GCE was needed, I was motivated to examine women's leadership for GCE through the lens of critical pedagogy to reinvent Freire's[1] concept of citizenship along the dimension of race and gender. Through critical inquiry, I wanted to understand as Freire (1994) encouraged us to do, how to move beyond the ability of *reading the word*, to include *reading the world*. Friere asks educators to go beyond literacy, his reference to *reading the word*, to providing students with critical tools for understanding the dynamics of power and justice in their world, hence *reading the world* (Freire & Macedo, 1995). Female students in my classes come primarily from the Global South, including East Asia, South Asia, Southeast Asia, and South America. Often, they are reluctant to acknowledge the validity of their lived experiences in *reading the world*. My challenge is to work toward bringing Freire's (1998) words to life as he shared, "My presence *in* the world, *with* the world, and *with* other people implies my complete knowledge of myself ... [to] understand myself in such completeness ... it will be possible for me to make history, knowing that I too am made by history" (p. 52). This calls for a process of dynamic self-awareness, and I questioned how to best activate this process with my students. While focusing on the intersectionality of race, ethnicity, and gender, there was a desire to "constructively transform that awareness and outrage into action, into a global sense of solidarity for justice" (Arnot, 2009, p. 124). Critical pedagogy thus emerged as a pathway for the inclusion of a gendered perspective in GCE, activating a process of empowerment (Guajardo & Vohra, 2023). CP is further explained below as a space for reimaging a better future.

Critical Global Citizenship Education

Views on global citizenship education range from equality and charity to equity and justice (Pluim, et al., 2014). Moving from equality to equity requires examining the complexity of local/global processes rooted in inequalities of power (Andreotti, 2006). These inequalities undergird both the definition and strategy of *critical* GCE. The word critical does not refer to right or wrong or a critique of GCE; rather, it holds the space for developing critical engagement and reflexivity skills. An important first step is to examine the purpose of GCE (Bruce, North & Fitzpatrick, 2019). If the purpose remains unexamined and GCE is seen as abstract elements of a common humanity, disregarding the imbalance of power, GCE will elude the possibility of meaningful engagement (Ellsworth, 1989).

Critical GCE aims to "empower individuals to reflect critically on the legacies and processes of their cultures, to imagine different futures, and to take responsibility for decisions and actions" (Andreotti, 2006, p. 48). Within *critical* GCE, reimagining the concept of power and encouraging learners to connect to one's voice and to their lived experiences is vital. Empowering students allows them to "courageously step into their vulnerability, to connect to and deepen their understanding of themselves, in order to then approach the other … to make meaning of the process and their experience of the 'other'" (Giroux & Bosio, 2021, p. 9). To undertake this deeper understanding of themselves, students are required to engage in a process of unlearning, relearning, and learning familiar concepts. What did power, leadership, and agency mean to them? What new and reimagined views might emerge?

Critical Pedagogy

Critical pedagogy (CP), as introduced by Freire (1970), is based on a social justice lens and suggests that students are not empty containers but, in fact, bring their hopes, challenges, and lived experiences to a learning space. The focus is directed at empowerment and citizenship, where teachers and students create a space that fosters critical inquiry, agency, and awareness, leading to action. Simply stated, "Critical pedagogy as a field confronts this gap between what is and what could be and all the social inequalities that produce it" (Gore, 2015, p. 81). It identifies principles of practice that aim to increase equity as opposed to outlining a definitive list of teaching strategies. CP thus became my foundation for *critical* GCE.

My own educational approach brought together these principles of practice to embrace an approach that bell hooks says requires "expanding beyond to imagine and enact pedagogical practices that engage ... biases in curricula that reinscribe systems of domination (such as racism and sexism) while simultaneously providing new ways to teach diverse groups of students" (1994, p. 10). As a professor, my goal is to create a learning space of possibility. This requires designing teaching strategies that allow female and male students to feel safe, to reach across differences, and to incorporate a spirit of belonging so that a generic sense of unity does not wash out the differences in lived experiences. Embracing the complexity of our experiences without fear, shame, or blame would contribute to a sense of wholeness. Our work necessitated heightening our level of comfort with complexity and not trying to reduce the world to a simple checklist. As hooks (1994) shares, to "have a transformative impact ... [to] engage in open critical dialogue with one another, where we can debate and discuss without fear ... where we can hear and know one another in the difference and complexities of our experience" (p. 110). Cultivating a questioning mind and interrupting existing power dynamics allow for this reimaging and co-creating to occur.

To interrupt existing power relationships in the classroom, the learning experience must be relevant to students' lives and refrain from bending toward abstraction (Ellsworth, 1989). This requires connecting learning to historical and political contexts, inviting lived experiences into the learning space, "urging all of us to open our minds and hearts ... so that we can think and rethink, so that we can create new visions [to] celebrate teaching that enables transgressions—a movement against and beyond boundaries" (hooks, 1994, p. 12). Misiaszek (2023) calls this work the deepening and widening of perspectives for both students and teachers, an approach of critical inquiry that teaches students how to think, not what to think. In the process of unlearning, relearning, and learning, students learn to question, disassemble, and integrate their understanding of the world, developing the capacity to reclaim and revise their sense of self and their understanding of identity, leadership, and power.

The inclusion of a gendered GCE perspective requires reaching and engaging across differences. Through building trust and allowing one's vulnerability to emerge, students learn to connect their head and heart. Challenging learners to connect with critical questions "fosters the heart of the learner and advances social justice and sustainability for all communities" (Torres & Bosio, 2020, p. 110). "Another classroom is possible ... we cannot create that other world, that world where many worlds fit, unless we first create another classroom, one in which all voices and lives count" (Armbruster-Sandoval, 2005, p. 34). The question then is how to create this other classroom where all lives count, and GCE becomes inclusive and gendered by design rather than by default.

Principles of Practice

Reading Critically

Freire asks educators to go beyond literacy, his reference to *reading the word*, to providing students with critical tools for understanding the dynamics of power and justice in their world, hence *reading the world* (Freire & Macedo, 1995).

Critical pedagogy principles of practice have emerged in my teaching experience, demonstrating promise in supporting students in *reading the world*. Through a process of trial and error, these principles of practice informed teaching strategies that awakened students to their sense of power and self-determination to embody roles as change agents, leaders, and global citizens. This chapter will present three teaching strategies: *reconceptualizing power*, *integrating lived narratives*, and *transformational dialog*. All three strategies served to activate a process of self-awareness, critical inquiry, and an empowering praxis.

Students explored complex dimensions of their identity by confronting the hidden, the unchallenged, and the uncomfortable. Placing students at the center as subjects through reflection, critical inquiry, dialog, and a process of reimagination, a new relationship with self, others, power, and leadership was crafted. Through this learning experience, students chose critical awareness over ignorance. Their words and actions revealed unprecedented agency and a renewed commitment to social change.

Reconceptualizing Power

Students engaged in reconceptualizing the concept of power from negative to purposeful. It was evident that these opportunities to question, reframe, and integrate new ways of being and knowing were altering students' understanding of their own sense of agency. Through readings and exercises, students began to question what they knew, including the cultural norms they were raised within their family and community and their views of leadership and power. Questioning and reflecting on power dynamics is central to CP, as noted by Mohanty (1989), "*A number of educators, Paulo Freire among them, have argued that education represents both a struggle for meaning and a struggle over power relations*" (p. 184). Students, when given license to redefine the concept of power through interactive exercises, focused on power *with* others not power *over* others.

Integrating Lived Narratives

To connect the texts to the students' diverse experiences, students were invited to structure a learning space to share their own experiences. Connecting to students' lived narratives increased the relevancy of the class content as students discovered that their story was just as valid as any other and deserved to be heard. One student shared in a final class reflection:

> If I want to understand where race and gender, or race and age, or gender and class, intersect, I need to make it personal. If I want to feel enraged and motivated to take action, I need to personalize it … Being part of the solution means exactly this, to personalize and then put into practice the learning from this class, and understand that change starts now, it starts where I am, and it starts with me.

In addition to personalizing the learning experience, students needed to discover their own voice. Speaking to others and sharing one's experience empowered students to feel that their voice and story mattered.

Transformational Dialog

Throughout my teaching experience, dialog has become a tool central to building trust and community. It is a teaching strategy that can engage students in connecting with themselves and others. Transformational dialog is different from everyday conversation. As Freire (1970) shares, dialog is not a ping-pong match where two individuals go back and forth. Dialog requires deep listening and a willingness to change as a result of this listening.

Furthermore, I have come to understand that spaces for dialog are not neutral. Individuals from marginalized communities assess the risk and cost of what is/can be said to whom and in what context (Ellsworth, 1989). Disclosure necessitates being seen by others, and this occurs through a "highly complex negotiation of the politics of knowing and being known" (p. 313). The issues of trust, fear, risk, and desire around issues of identity and politics in the classroom are real and must be addressed. For students to allow themselves to be seen and included, they must trust and believe that they can define themselves as authors of their own world.

The purpose of engaging and reflecting positions students to engage in a process of discovery, of pushing back, of reevaluating traditions that leave them silent and invisible. As noted by hooks (1986) "true speaking is not solely an expression of creative power, it is an act of resistance, a political gesture that challenges the politics of domination that would render us nameless and voiceless ... it is a courageous act" (p. 126). As students looked forward to a future course of action, their reflections spoke of a strengthening commitment.

These three teaching strategies—reconceptualizing power, integrating lived narratives, and transformational dialog—illustrate how CP principles of practice began to expand the narrative of global citizenship, women, and leadership.

Conclusion

Freire's written work from *Pedagogy of the Oppressed* (1970) to *Pedagogy of Hope* (1994) captures an evolution of thought, a reinvention of beliefs and practices that became more meaningful with time. Deepening and widening students' understanding of social justice and social change through critical pedagogy provides the tools for transformation (Misiaszek, 2023). As an awakening of consciousness continues to emerge, both in myself and in my students, I have experienced how critical pedagogy is a pathway for praxis, connecting theory to action. When lived through the lens of critical pedagogy, global citizenship, women, and leadership are disruptive and push one to the margins of the academy. This presents a quagmire for GCE in universities that have typically championed an approach more closely aligned with a neoliberal, male-dominated view.

Critical pedagogy requires weighing the risks and benefits of speaking up and speaking out. Ellsworth (1989) warns us not to fall prey to magical thinking, "Acting as if our classroom were a safe space in which democratic dialogue was possible and happening did not make it so" (p. 315). Teaching and learning practices that confront the power dynamics in systems and structures will launch an educational renaissance. To close with the words of bell hooks (1994), "it takes a fierce commitment, a will to struggle, to let our work … reflect progressive pedagogies" (p. 143). This fierce commitment on behalf of students, teachers, and the community is both individual and collective. It is time to reimagine education as a place for building community based on deep trust and commitment to a more inclusive world. Another classroom is possible, and this will lead to a change in the world, building an educational system where the inclusion of voices is normalized, continually examining its purpose and power.

Note

1   A Brazilian educator from the Global South, in contrast to the Global North perspective.

References

Andreotti, V. (2006). Soft versus critical global citizenship education. *Development Education Review*. Derry: Centre for Global Education. https://www.developmenteducationreview.com/issue/issue-3/soft-versus-critical-global-citizenship-education.

Armbruster-Sandoval, R. (2005). Is another world possible? Is another classroom possible? Radical pedagogy, activism, and social change. *Social Justice*, 32(2 (100)), 34–51. San Francisco, CA: Social Justice Publishing Collective. http://www.jstor.org/stable/29768306.

Arnot, M. (2009). A global conscience collective? Incorporating gender injustices into global citizenship education. *Education, Citizenship and Social Justice SAGE Publications*, 4(2), 117–32. London: SAGE Publications. https://doi.org/10.1177/1746197909103932.

Bruce, J., North, C., & FitzPatrick, J. (2019). Preservice teachers' views of global citizenship and implications for global citizenship education. *Globalisation, Societies and Education*, 17(2), 161–76. Abingdon: Taylor & Francis. https://doi.org/10.1080/14767724.2018.1558049.

Ellsworth, E. (1989). Why doesn't this feel empowering? Working through the repressive myths of critical pedagogy. *Harvard Educational Review*, 59(3), 297–324. Cambridge, MA: Harvard Education Publishing Group.

Freire, P. (1970). *Pedagogy of the oppressed*. New York, NY: Seabury.

Freire, P. (1994). *Pedagogy of hope: Reliving pedagogy of the oppressed*. New York, NY: Continuum.

Freire, P. (1998). *Teachers as cultural workers: Letters to those who dare teach*. Boulder, CO: Westview Press.

Freire, P., & Macedo, D. (1995). A dialogue: Culture, language, and race. *Harvard Educational Review*, 65(3), 377–402. Cambridge, MA: Harvard Education Publishing Group.

Giroux, H. A., & Bosio, E. (2021). Critical pedagogy and global citizenship education. In E. Bosio (Ed.), *Conversations on global citizenship education: Perspectives on research, teaching, and learning in higher education* (pp. 1–10). New York, NY: Routledge.

Gore, J. (2015). My struggle for pedagogy. In B. Porfilio, & D. Ford (Eds.), *Leaders in critical pedagogy: Narratives for understanding and solidarity* (pp. 81–91). Rotterdam: Sense Publishers.

Guajardo, M., & Vohra, S. (2023). Linking global citizenship education and critical pedagogy: Women's leadership and power. *Citizenship Teaching and Learning*, 18(2), 159–75. Bristol: Intellect Ltd. https://doi.org/10.1386/ctl_00118_1.

hooks, b. (1986). Talking back. *Discourse*, 8, 123–8. Melbourne: Monash University Publishing (Discourse origin, though now often associated with Taylor & Francis). http://www.jstor.org/stable/44000276.

hooks, b. (1994). *Teaching to transgress: Education as the practice of freedom*. New York, NY: Routledge.

Misiaszek, G. W. (2023). *Freire and environmentalism: Ecopedagogy*. New York, NY: Bloomsbury Academic.

Mohanty, C. T. (1989). On race and voice: Challenges for liberal education in the 1990s. *Cultural Critique*, 14, 179–208. Minneapolis, MN: University of Minnesota Press. https://doi.org/10.2307/1354297.

Northhouse, P. (2017). *Introduction leadership: Concepts and practice* (4th ed.). Thousand Oaks, CA: Sage Publications.

Pluim, G., MacDonald, A., & Niyozov, S. (2014). Bend without breaking: Applying critical reflexive practice in global citizenship education. In D. Montemurro, M. Gambhir, M. Evans, & K. Broad (Eds.), *Inquiry into practice: Learning and teaching global matters in local classrooms* (pp. 115–20). Toronto: Ontario Institute for Studies in Education of the University of Toronto.

Tormey, R. & Gleeson, J. (2012). The gendering of global citizenship: Findings from a large-scale quantitative study on global citizenship education experiences. *Gender and Education*, 24(6), 627–45, Abingdon: Taylor & Francis. https://doi.org/10.1080/09540253.2011.646960.

Torres, C. A., & Bosio, E. (2020). Global citizenship education at the crossroads: Globalization, global commons, common good, and critical consciousness. *Prospects*, 48(3), 99–113. Dordrecht: Springer. https://doi.org/10.1007/s11125-019-09458-w.

CHAPTER EIGHT

Freire in the Classroom as Ecopedagogy in Higher Education Settings

Cae Rodrigues

Early Inspirations and Embodied Praxis

Freire has always been an influence. My mother was a teacher and used Freire's method of alphabetization in her classes and with her children, so Freire's ideals of a caring and dialogical education have always been present at home. The very same ideals are still present in my daily life today, in my interactions with my friends and my students, with the grocery owner when I go shopping and with the doorman in my building, with my partner and my daughter at home. This is what praxis[1] is all about: Thinking a certain way does not lead to acting a certain way; thought and action is one holistic construct.

So, when asked about how Freire's work is present in my work as a teacher and a researcher, I could say I use Freire's concepts of "generative themes," "knowledge from experience," "meaningful learning," "critical political engagement," and "affectivity as education" as academic references and "pedagogical tools," as these concepts certainly are present as references to my research and teaching pedagogies. But it's much more than that, because I don't use these concepts as pedagogical tools—I share my living experiences of these (incorporated; embodied) concepts with the students in/as interactive ways of learning.

In trying to live up to the challenging idea of ecological praxis, work becomes but an extension of my readings of the world, of how I perceive the idea of what can be called "ecological" and how I act upon this idea. And how I construct these ecological readings of the world is, of course, intrinsically related to my studies on the topic. So my environmental pedagogical work, be it teaching classes in the university, or doing research to develop ecopedagogies, or giving courses to environmental educators in the Amazon, all of this is me sharing this aesthetic-ethical-political construct that I live as praxis, while learning in the interactions with the individuals (humans and nonhumans) that are part of these encounters. In this dialogical process, an environment of co-creative knowledge is built, where learning is the praxis of incorporating that which makes sense to me, to my readings of the world, in my world context. And that's deeply connected to Freirean theory.

Freire and Environmental Pedagogies

The influence of Freire's work on environmental pedagogies is remarkable. This is especially true in Latin America, where Freire's work has had a greater historical influence on education theory, having a direct effect on teacher formation and, thus, teaching practices. In Brazil, for example, the influence of Freire's work is certainly one of the main reasons to why environmental education has been consolidated as the predominant environmental pedagogical current, instead of education for sustainable development or sustainability education, for example, which are powered by influential institutions, such as the United Nations and the private sector, and are more common predominant currents in countries of the Global North (Rodrigues & Arenas, 2022). Moreover, considering how diversified the field of environmental education[2] has become (e.g., see Sauvé's typology from 2005 describing fifteen different currents of environmental education almost two decades ago), the predominant current in Brazil is "critical environmental education," which is directly connected to Freirean theory (Carvalho, 2004).

The predominance of critical environmental education among the many options of environmental pedagogies and, more specifically, the different currents or "strands" of environmental education, is a decolonial political stance (Carvalho, 2002; Rodrigues & Arenas, 2022). Looking back at this history is also key to understanding the current rise of "ecopedagogy" as a growingly influential environmental pedagogy in Brazil (Rodrigues & Silva, 2023), and also beyond Latin American borders as publications about ecopedagogy in the English language start to pile up (e.g., Payne, 2018; Misiaszek, 2020). As even critical environmental education starts to take on too much in terms of purposes and aims, ecopedagogy rises, again as a political stance of decolonial resistance, also based on Freire's critical pedagogy, but with a more defined focus on "ecological" values (ecoaesthetics-environmental ethics-ecopolitics as an inseparable triad—see Payne et al., 2018).

To further acknowledge this important history and, in so doing, minimizing the risk of "historical amnesia"[3] that has become (too) common in the fast track of academic production (Payne, 2020), the main difference of ecopedagogy from the lot of environmental theories and pedagogical currents out there is how radical ecopedagogy is in its focus and in its propositions (see Dickmann, 2022). Environmental education was quite radical in its initial propositions, if we go back to the first agendas coming out of Stockholm and Tbilisi and if we look back at the genesis of the environmental movement, contextualized within the wave of countercultural movements of the 1960s and 1970s that said: "enough! The structure we live in is unjust and we need to change" (Rodrigues & Arenas, 2022). But environmental education ended up taking too much along the years (going back to Sauvé's fifteen currents already back in 2005). So this is where ecopedagogy's strength lies on its radicalness: It has in Paulo Freire a central reference, and that makes its goals and, just as important, its limitations much clearer and more acknowledgeable.

Also, these goals are very timely and up to date. They target the built-in structures of capitalism and of unjust human relations that are still incrusted in our institutions and naturalized in our bodies that are expressed as forms of anthropocentrism, patriarchy, colonialism (Dickmann, 2022). And they call for affectivity in the form of a caring and loving education. Basically, if you are educated through violence, be it physical or symbolic, you will learn and reproduce violence. On the other hand, if you learn through caring and love, you will learn and reproduce care and love toward everything. Ecological learning is not about learning to care for nature, it's just about learning to care for everything—caring for nature is a consequence. So the message in ecopedagogy is very clear and, as such, very powerful: If education does not tackle the problems of capitalism and of unjust social structures, it cannot be understood as ecological.

In the Classroom

To take this discussion to the classroom, I will focus on an account of the disciplinary unit "Physical education and environment," taught by me since 2014 at the Federal University of Sergipe (UFS), in the Northeast of Brazil. The aim of the unit is to discuss the possibilities and limitations of developing environmental pedagogies as a physical education professional. It is an elective unit under the title of a "special topic," but it will become compulsory in the next curricular implementation at the physical education department at

UFS (expected for 2025). The new curricular proposal will also offer an elective unit on "Nature sports and recreation," more focused on (de)(re)constructing the (Eurocentric; gender biased; elitist) historical imaginaries of sport and leisure in relation to ecopedagogical possibilities (and limitations) (Rodrigues, 2019). These changes are, in great part, a result from government mandates that are pushing for the inclusion of "environment" as a transversal theme in all disciples and all levels of education in Brazil, one of the main guidelines from the Brazilian Politics of Environmental Education, a document from 1999 (Rodrigues, 2023).

In the classroom, we start things off deconstructing: Students conjure their life experiences (readings of the world—Freire, 1996) to define their own meaning(s) of nature, environment, conservation, sustainability, and development, a process where their knowledge from experience (Freire, 1996) is acknowledged and valued. The first discussions happen within smaller groups, driven by generative themes (Freire, 1981) projected to challenge naturalized imaginaries, or collective representations. After each group has elaborated a collective (re)conceptualization for each of the given concepts (reconstruction), we go on to discuss how these representations are conceived: Where do they come from? What are the main influences in their genesis? How are they related to their family culture, to their local/regional/national cultures, or other influences to their readings of the world? Have they changed during their lifetime, how and why? How do they influence their daily lives and inter-actions with other human and nonhuman beings and environments? Are they anthropocentric, biocentric, or ecocentric? Are they socially and environmentally just?

Only after this long line of questioning as an exercise of (phenomenological) deconstruction (see Payne & Wattchow, 2009; Rodrigues, 2015), a series of scientific articles are chosen, by the groups, to integrate the process of conceptualization according to their potential to reinforce or contest the formulated representations. The groups are free to research and suggest articles that can potentially dialog with their (re) constructed representations (one class is set up in a way to help the groups with this research in the University library, but they can of course extend the research on their own). Articles can also be chosen from a shared folder organized by the teacher containing a large array of manuscripts from the environmental (education) field and that more specifically address the synergies between physical education and environmental pedagogies (including, but in no way limited to, those associated to outdoor and adventure education).

This critical work of conceptualization is constantly supported by contextualization in praxis, which can happen in a number of proposed ways which the students can freely

FIGURE 8.1 *Students interviewing surfer in field research to support their conceptual representations (personal archives)*

FIGURE 8.2 *Forest trails are an example of the group experiences in different environments to challenge students to praxically acknowledge possibilities, limits, and "silences" of their conceptual representations (personal archives)*

choose from (as well as other possibilities suggested by the groups, and discussed among everyone, along the way). Examples include: Elaboration of "manifestos for a sustainable life," or "manifestos for ecological biographies of movement," connecting (and respectively evolving as) written "manifesto of ideals" that emerge from their conceptual representations, mind maps showing the interrelated nature of the proposed ideals, and plans for action to exercise the proposed ideals in chosen (local) "places" (a neighborhood, school, social project, etc.); field research in different environments that might support their conceptual representations, where they can collect data through direct observations, interviews, field diaries, moving ethnographies, etc.; group experiences in different environments to challenge them to praxically acknowledge possibilities, limits, and "silences" of their conceptual representations; "ecomotricity labs" (Rodrigues, 2018), where the groups elaborate ecopedagogical workshops for "moving in nature as ecological praxis" based on their conceptual representations (group dynamics for the workshops can be elaborated by the students or chosen from an array of dynamics available in a shared folder). As the groups are involved in these practices they can modify or incorporate new elements to their collective representations, constantly confronting text and context, or contrasting "readings of the world" and "readings of the word" (Freire, 1996).

Forest trails are an example of the group experiences in different environments to challenge students to praxically acknowledge possibilities, limits, and "silences" of their conceptual representations (personal archives)

Toward the end of the semester, a public meeting is co-organized by the students and teacher at the University (extension project) to which colleagues, students from other areas, and people from outside the University community (including those that were involved in the contextualization experiences described in the previous paragraph) are invited to attend. In this meeting the students present their findings of the semester as a research project presentation in poster or oral communication format. The rule is that some form of empirical data needs to be presented, which the students will have collected from the contextualization experiences. The empirical data also needs to dialog with the bibliography that was chosen to support the discussions during the semester.

FIGURE 8.3 *Students presenting their "manifestos for a sustainable life" in the end of semester public meeting (personal archives)*

During the presentations in the public meeting, the students are susceptible to different worldviews, questions, and critics (they are also encouraged to raise questions and formulate critiques regarding the work of their colleagues). The possibility of dialoguing, criticizing, doubting, and concurring pushes the students to, once again, reflect and question their own concepts (Freire, 1992). This "exposure" is, thus, not only valuable as part of the process of (phenomenological) conceptualization, but also key as representation and legitimation of the experientially constructed knowledge. Looking back at the whole process, conceptualization, contextualization, and re-presentation are put together aiming meaningful knowledge construction and political action. It is, above all, a process of empowerment.

The decade-long experience of the (eco)pedagogical journey described in the last pages have also shown how the proposed dynamics are malleable and adaptable to the waves of time and context, as well as suitable and pertinent to students from different academic fields. Since the process is mostly constructed through participatory and collaborative exchanges, it is, in great part, wrought and shaped by the personal histories of the actors involved. As an elective unit, it is common to have students that are in different stages of their undergraduate courses, as well as students from different academic disciplines (not only Physical Education). So even though the initial outline of the course is pretty much the same year in and year out, the actual syllabus and the praxis of the course is quite different from year to year.

Relevant Considerations ...

I've been asked in more than one opportunity about the "changes" I see during the semester regarding student's environmental "awareness." Having experienced the pedagogical methodology described in the previous section a good number of times in the last decade, I can answer this question with a certain level of confidence: The final constructs about important concepts in the environmental field (nature, environment, conservation, sustainability, development) presented by most groups at the end of the semester are drastically different from their initial representations; however, they are still generally bound to concepts and discourses associated to historically fashioned trends in experiences in nature and romanticized body–environment relations (see chapter 2 in Rodrigues, 2019). But that's fine, and expected, if we look back at Fay's (1987) description of the ontological limits to change.

The aim is not reaching "environmentally friendly" or "(eco)politically correct" pre-determined concepts or ways of thinking and acting that serves a particular cause. This is how we fall into the trap of a normative and instrumental "banking" education (Freire, 1981) that weighs as responsibility what it lacks in meaningfulness. Responsibility that should not be equally distributed among people from very different social contexts, as not everyone has the same socioenvironmental conditions to comply with them. Thus, the aim of the described pedagogical methodology is not so much on the product, but rather on the process of understanding that concepts are socially built. This understanding is kindled by different ways of being-with-others, humans and nonhumans (we place ourselves in the world as we interact with all that is "not-us"— Freire, 1996), and by different provocations for meaningful (de)(re)constructions (ex)posed as personal aesthetics-ethics-politics (Payne et al., 2018)—ways of thinking and acting (being!) in the world, thus, paths to empowerment.

So it's not really about the "changes," as more is generally needed for change than the few months in an academic semester or the scholastic structure of a curricular unit (see Rodrigues, 2018). It's not about "awareness" either, as this is not taught, but spawned in slow, time-demanding, culturally conditioned (yet, not determined) praxis (Freire, 1996). It's much more about (re)discoveries within generative corporeal dissonances (phenomenological deconstructions)[4] within different ways of being-in-the-world that can, potentially, lead to ecological praxis.

In relevant considerations, acknowledging limitations is always key. I always feel the theory–practice gap is a tough remaining challenge. The positive legitimation of the environmental discourse and the consequent processes of environmentalization (Lopes, 2006), or greening, in our society are very important. We see it everywhere: In education, in construction, in our laws, in the ways we, as a society, enjoy our free time. But the remaining gaps between (theoretical) prescriptions and (practical) descriptions are still too great. Another difficult challenge is scoping ecological pedagogies beyond what is proposed by discourses such as sustainability or sustainable development, more widely "available." We need to acknowledge the importance of these discourses in advancing the environmental cause, of course, but we need to also understand what they lack in ecopedagogy, and the unsustainable structures they help to perpetuate (as well highlighted in the works of Ingolf Bluhdorn, Greg Misziazeck, Phillip Payne, Helen Kopnina, Arjen Wells, just to cite a few).

But, to end on a positive note, I try to remain optimistic. There are good signs out there of an aesthetic shift that is important, people really wanting to spend more time in nature, which could be a driving force for both environmental conservation and ecological consciousness as people learn-with the environment. In education, we also see a growing space for environmental theories and methodologies based on meaningful learning of grounded knowledge, especially the kind of knowledge that challenges the injustices of the capitalist system, the patriarchy, and colonialism, such as Freirean-inspired ecopedagogy. The kind of knowledge that promotes a pedagogy of praxis through caring for other humans, for planet earth, and for life in its multiple manifestations.

Acknowledgments: This manuscript is dedicated to my grandparents (in memoriam), Ângela and Maurício (how they liked to be called), who never read Freire, but educated their children and their grandchildren through care and love. And to my mother, Isis (how she likes to be called), who found in her many readings of Freire a theoretical support to what she already practiced with her pupils, including her two children. I'm sure I can also speak for my sister and my father when I say she remains to be an inspiration to how beautiful life can be when we live it through thankfulness and love.

Notes

1   Praxis brings the understanding that theory (the embodiment of the aesthetically perceived world projected as "ideas") and

action (ethically driven politics based on these "ideas") are not, in any way, separate processes but a mutually designed artifact of body–world interactions.

2 Naming environmental education as a field means acknowledging its internal disputes, as, by and large, a social field is defined by the disputes surrounding particular capitals where positions of dominance are constantly at play (Bourdieu, 1989).

3 Academic tendency to producing "new" theory while not acknowledging the historical narratives of the field (see Payne, 2020; Rodrigues, 2020).

4 The concept of phenomenological deconstructions is deeply connected to the idea of experiences that challenge our "naturalized" or incorporated ways of being-in-the world (our automatized ways of thinking-acting). These experiences of "corporeal dissonance" that challenge our automatized ways of being-in-the-world, thus causing strangeness and stress, are key to the process of deconstructing that which is "naturalized." In this sense, they can be (potentially) generative to change (see Payne & Wattchow, 2009; Rodrigues, 2015).

References

Bourdieu, P. (1989). *O poder simbólico*. Rio de Janeiro: Bertrand Brasil.

Carvalho, I. C. M. (2002). O ambiental como valor substantivo: uma reflexão sobre a identidade da educação ambiental. In L. Sauvé, I. Orellana, & M. Sato (Eds.), *Textos escolhidos em educação ambiental: de uma América à outra* (pp. 85–90). Montreal: Publications ERE-UQAM (tomo I).

Carvalho, I. C. M. (2004). Educação ambiental crítica: nomes e endereçamentos da educação. In *Identidades da educação ambiental brasileira* (pp. 13–24). Brasília: MMA.

Dickmann, I. (2022). Reinventando a ecopedagogia: patriarcado, modernidade e capitalismo. *Revista Sergipana de Educação Ambiental*, 9(1), 1–16.

Fay, B. (1987). *Critical social science: Liberation and its limits*. New York, NY: Cornell University Press.

Freire, P. (1981). *Pedagogia do Oprimido* (10ᵃ ed.). Rio de Janeiro: Editora Paz, Terra.

Freire, P. (1992). *Pedagogy of the hope*. Sao Paulo: Paz e Terra.

Freire, P. (1996). *Pedagogia da autonomia: saberes necessários à prática educativa*. Rio de Janeiro, Brazil: Paz e Terra.

Lopes, J. S. L. (2006). Sobre processos de "ambientalização" dos conflitos e sobre dilemas da participação. *Horizontes Antropológicos*, 12(25), 31–64.

Misiaszek, G. W. (2020). *Ecopedagogy: Critical environmental teaching for planetary justice and global sustainable development*. London: Bloomsbury. www.bloomsbury.com/uk/ecopedagogy-9781350083813.

Payne, P. G. (2018). The framing of ecopedagogy as/in scapes: Methodology of the issue. *The Journal of Environmental Education*, 49(2), 71–87. doi: 10.1080/00958964.2017.1417227.

Payne, P. G. (2020). "Amnesia of the moment" in environmental education. *The Journal of Environmental Education*, 51(2), 113–43. doi: 10.1080/00958964.2020.1726263.

Payne, P. G., & Wattchow, B. (2009). Phenomenological deconstruction, slow pedagogy, and the corporeal turn in wild environmental/outdoor education. *Canadian Journal of Environmental Education*, 14, 15–32.

Payne, P., Rodrigues, C., Carvalho, I. C. M., Santos, L. M. F., Aguayo, C., & Iared, V. G. (2018). Affectivity in environmental education research. *Pesquisa em Educação Ambiental*, 13, 93–114.

Rodrigues, C. (2015). O *vagabonding* como estratégia pedagógica para a "desconstrução fenomenológica" em programas experienciais de educação ambiental. *Educação em revista*, 31(1), 303–27. doi: http://dx.doi.org/10.1590/0102-4698118598.

Rodrigues, C. (2018). MovementScapes as ecomotricity in ecopedagogy. *The Journal of Environmental Education*, 49(2), 88–102. doi:10.1080/00958964.2017.1417222.

Rodrigues, C. (2019). *Atividades alternativas e meio ambiente*. Londrina: Editora e Distribuidora Educacional S.A.

Rodrigues, C. (2020). What's new? Projections, prospects, limits and silences in "new" theory and "post" North–South representations. *The Journal of Environmental Education*, 51(2), 171–82. https://doi.org/10.1080/00958964.2020.1726267.

Rodrigues, C. (2023). Processos de ambientalização curricular e a base nacional comum curricular (BNCC): Idealismos, realidades e caminhos para a práxis generativa. In J. O. Dantas, & M. J. N. Soares (Eds.), *Conversação com educadores ambientais* (pp. 83–118). Aracaju: Criação Editora.

Rodrigues, C., & Arenas, A. (2022). Stockholm +50, Tbilisi +45, Rio +30: Research, praxis, and policy. *The Journal of Environmental Education*, 53(6), 309–13. doi: 10.1080/00958964.2022.2128016.

Rodrigues, C., & Silva, T. C. S. (2023). Ecomotricity of planting and caring: A decolonial and ecophenomenological pedagogical framework. *Motricidades*, 7(2), 92–104. doi: http://dx.doi.org/10.29181/2594-6463-2023-v7-n2-p92-104.

Sauvé, L. (2005). Uma cartografia das correntes em educação ambiental. In M. Sato, & I. C. M. Carvalho (Eds.), *Educação Ambiental: pesquisa e desafios* (pp. 17–46). Porto Alegre: Artmed.

CHAPTER NINE

Performing Policy—The Justice Project: Playing the Word in the World

Brent Blair

In his collaborative book with Donaldo Macedo, Paulo Freire noted that literacy is more than reading the world, it also requires "a certain form of writing it or rewriting it, that is, of transforming it by means of conscious, practical work" (1987, pp. 23–4). During the past five years, USC's School of Dramatic Arts and the Price School of Public Policy have collaborated with an innovative NGO called Healing Dialogue and Action (HDA) to help USC students read and then rewrite the oppressive narrative of the American carceral system. The USC class called Performing Policy: The Justice Project (PPJP) is the byproduct of this innovative collaboration.

The PJPP Course

The PPJP was the collective brainchild of the USC Price School of Public Policy professor David Sloane, PhD (Instructor,

PPD 400: Public Policy and Urban Studies) and the USC School of Dramatic Arts professor of practice Brent Blair, PhD (Instructor, THTR 488: Theatre in the Community) in conjunction with Javier Stauring, director of the restorative justice NGO HDA. It was designed to address a curricular gap common in some academic settings: that theory about contemporary social justice issues rarely translates into practice within the classroom space, and even more rarely are theory and practice treated together through the medium of live, interactive art. It is true that theater and social change courses have found a curricular home in higher education for decades; in fact, entire undergraduate and graduate programs have been dedicated to the theory and practice of a variety of models of this genre of art and activism, with an estimated eight undergraduate programs and another twenty-three graduate programs worldwide (Applied Theatre Programs, January 23, 2024). Typically, however, these programs teach the practice of theater and social change, but do not focus on particular issues or maintain multi-year partnerships where policy and performing arts classes partner with NGO advocacy organizations to place current policy issues into a public forum through the arts.

PPJP's unique focus on the theatrical praxis of justice goes beyond standard curricular instruction; it aims to shift policy, or at least transform public perceptions about the current policies surrounding criminal justice in California. The class responds to the current carceral crisis in the United States, which contains "only 4.4 percent of the global population, yet it holds nearly a quarter of the world's prisoners" (Anderson, 2019). Students, working with the HDA community partners whose lives have been directly impacted by violence, have been collaboratively rewriting this sociopolitical script on an annual basis since 2019, inviting audience members to observe, interact, and even further rewrite the narrative through what is known in Theatre of the Oppressed circles as "Forum Theatre."

Applying Pedagogy of the Oppressed

Freire's notion of *conscientization* (1985, p. 59) is everywhere present in the work of Theatre of the Oppressed, codified by the late Augusto Boal, a friend and colleague of Freire's for many decades. Just as Freire exhorts the reader to engage critically with the written word and rewrite it according to their own needs and desires, so Boal's methodology invites spectators to become "spect-actors" and invade the theatrical space, replacing protagonists in the scene and re-imagining the scripted dialog of oppression using new strategies (Boal, 1992, p. 15). The audience is interrogated throughout the process, turning what typically is a theatrical monologue into a true experiential dialog, a "forum" (p. 23).

The PPJP experience foregrounds the dual instruction of theater and policy to "explore the tension between criminal justice and restorative justice (RJ) as policy and planning alternatives" (Sloane, 2024) and to "explore the theory and practice of liberating communities from … oppression through the vehicle of public performative art and expressive cultural dialogue" (Blair, 2024). By combining these two courses, a new shared objective becomes activated: the creation of a public artistic interactive dialog on the issue of Restorative Justice toward the goal of creating lasting social justice transformation.

Theatre of the Oppressed

Augusto Boal, Brazilian theater director and social activist, is the founder of **Theatre of the Oppressed** (TO), a methodology of liberatory philosophy dedicated to the notions of dialog, cooperative education, and the transformative potential of theater. Influenced by Paolo Freire's philosophy of education, TO performances activate passive spectators to become spect-actors, engaged participants rehearsing strategies for personal and social change.

Unlike many academic models[1] where Theatre of the Oppressed (TO) is embedded in the curriculum, the PPJP experience does not principally aim to teach the theory and practice of TO, but rather to utilize the tools of TO in the production of lasting policy transformation pertinent to the criminal justice system. For this reason, the frame is consistently on restorative justice, working steadily with the same community partner, even as student populations change from year to year. This consistency foregrounds the desire for consistent attention to a singular issue, bringing into focus the outcome objective of social change and policy transformation rather than imparting curricular information about theater and social change or public policy alone.

The prolific works of Paulo Freire and Augusto Boal share a basic core methodology that of the humanizing power of dialog as a force of resistance to oppressive, top-down systems. For Freire, the educational system was a symptom of the corrupt nature of oppressive systems that employ monolog as the means of content delivery. The only path to freedom is through restructuring systems to be based in dialog. For Freire, "Dialogue with the people is radically necessary to every authentic revolution" (Freire, 1970, p. 128); and as Boal put it, "Dialogue is Democracy" (1979/2000, p. xvi). In the spirit of both Theatre and the Pedagogy of the Oppressed, the PPJP experience promotes dialog through mindful play and creative collaboration, but while it also engages in rigorous research about the justice system, it does not pretend to provide answers or even speculate on expert analysis of this system without the constant presence of collective community, interactive inquiry. Restorative Justice is a process invested in reviving dialog between and among survivors and perpetrators of violence, predicated on the notion of deep reflection, critical inquiry, and collective action. This cyclical process is a parallel of Freire's notion of *conscientization*—a process of deep observation, critical reflection, and social action.

Applying Theatre of the Oppressed

The theme of Restorative Justice (RJ) is unique among topics about justice insofar as it rather precariously navigates traumatic stories of loss and violence. In *Changing Lenses,* his seminal book on Restorative Justice, author Howard Zehr observes:

> Crime is a violation of people and relationships. It creates obligations to make things right. Justice involves the victim, the offender, and the community in a search for solutions which promote repair, reconciliation, and reassurance.
>
> (Zehr, 1990, pp. 183–4)

As relationships between victim, offender, and community are intertwined, so too are their stories closely woven together. In the current PPJP 2024 project, one of the protagonists is an individual who traumatically lost a family member to violence, after which he participated in retributive violence for which there was further loss of lives. In such a fragile environment, the way risky stories are shared, witnessed, and then ultimately represented "craves wary walking" (Shakespeare, *Julius Caesar*, Act 2, Scene 1). Having a trauma-informed platform in place has been essential for both the students' and the community partners' safety. To support this platform, the PPJP class first uses Image Theater techniques[2] to reduce the risk of misinterpretation of traumatic stories which can, itself, be re-traumatizing. By taking time to collectively observe the embodied essence of a story through the participation of the students and partners in the room, all may behold the image and, without first dissecting its meaning, allow the image to speak in subtle ways to each observer's heart.

Image Theater

The first use of Image Theater in the PPJP course happens within the first few weeks of the semester. Students and volunteers alike are engaged in exercises leading to the creation of multiple embodied images whose purpose is to establish community agreements by asking the question, "what conditions within the workshop might make us feel trusted/untrusted." Mixed teams of four or five students and partners create *tableaux vivants* without words to demonstrate conditions of trust or distrust. These various images are then shared with the larger cohort and speculative evaluation opens up a democratic conversation about what we collectively may need to build a brave space for risky storytelling. As witnesses to the *tableaux* offer descriptive words they may associate with each image, their language is being recorded on a whiteboard for all to see. These lists of words, categorized as per the images by either "trust" or "mistrust," help reveal to the community at large what is possibly needed from each of us to ensure that an atmosphere of maximum trust is maintained in the working space.

Healing Circles

Healing circles are group dialogs where participants, seated in a circle, may all observe each other and speak in a space of shared leadership, empathy, and respect. Based on indigenous methods, they serve as valuable tools within restorative practices, creating an environment that fosters healing when harm is caused.

The next use of Image Theater focuses on building the world of the protagonist(s), and in our case, the three volunteers all formerly incarcerated and currently released members of the "wounded healer" teams at HDA. For this portion of the course, the volunteers were foregrounded and the students were asked to play auxiliary, supportive roles. It is perhaps useful to illuminate the PPJP course ethics by explaining the concept, inspired by Freire's premise that only oppressed can truly participate in their own liberating narratives (1970/2000, p. 56). This is a principle we refer to as "The Praxis of Proximity," that is, the more proximate the creator/storyteller is to the content of the story being presented, the more authentic their knowledge of the issue. While all opinions are welcome, they are not equal in weight; to avoid the pitfalls of individuals speaking knowledgeably on topics with which they are little familiar, the instructors of PPJP clarify that those most proximate to a theme must be given priority even if not exclusivity in sharing their narrative. The HDA partners, therefore, were most proximate to the experience of Restorative Justice as each had been incarcerated for more than ten years, each had experienced violence as both survivors and former offenders, and each had been a participant for multiple years in healing circles and the process of intense restorative justice dialogs.

Three prompts were provided and the HDA partners sculpted PPJP students into group statues in *tableaux vivants* to invite collective analysis and engagement to the story. First, they were asked to create statues revealing "how it was"— that is, what childhood experiences did the partners think most informed their path toward the experiences of violence, incarceration, and healing? Next, partners were asked to create status revealing "what happened"—that is, to show still images of the crime scene that led to the loss of life and ultimately their incarceration. Lastly, they spoke about their experiences of transformation. On this topic, it was decided not to invite student engagement in statue creation and interpretation as the specific and subtle nature of transformation for each partner must be expressed by their own experience without the opportunity to misinterpret or misunderstand their story.

Pairing community partners who are "family survivors of homicide, incarcerated and formerly incarcerated people, and communities affected by violent crime" (Homepage, 2021) with undergraduate students largely unfamiliar with this narrative requires an ethical frame. Author and critical theorist Julie Salverson refers to these narratives as "risky stories" (1996). Such a creative collaboration with sensitive material can prove ethically challenging, for both academics and artists: how is the spirit of criticality and dialog balanced within a framework of respect for the storyteller's perspective? Is there room for disagreement and discourse when the source story is sensitive, even traumatic, in content? Finally, what scenes can be treated as a "forum,"[3] and what scenes are considered too sensitive or traumatizing to allow audience participation? For the PPJP community, it was decided that the most risky stories would be shielded from audience interactive participation. We would come to label this group of stories as the "hearts and minds thread," described later.

Using Image Theater invites a particular autonomy to the creator of the image, and although students not proximate to the issue are invited to speculate on the finished *tableaux*, the final word is always given to its sculptor, the holder of the risky story. In this way, students are encouraged to enter into the risky situation to the extent they are able or willing without imposing their own perspectives in any conclusive or concrete way. Based on our work with the three HDA volunteers, the class generated powerful content that would supply material for many scenes throughout the play. This work also helped inform other scenes dealing with policy issues.

The Play Structure—Three Threads

In order to meet the complex goals imagined by the PPJP experience, it would be vital for the final product to meet a variety of objectives. First and foremost, the play would need to respect the lived experiences of those most proximate to its stories in order to humanize the issue of Restorative Justice

(RJ) and its impact on the lives of people inside and outside of the carceral system. As mentioned before, we have labeled this narrative the **"hearts and minds thread"** of our collective story. Within this thread we tell the story of the three HDA volunteers through their own words, treated primarily as poetry and monologues. Next, we needed to understand the core conditions of oppression that serve as obstacles to Restorative Justice, particularly within the State of California. For this, the policy students do extensive research on a broad range of topics pertinent to RJ which are translated into Forum Theatre scenes, a theme we refer to as the **"policy thread."** Finally, it is clear there are aspects of the criminal justice system with which the invited audience will be largely unfamiliar, and in order to provide essential information during the play, we have created the construct of commercials, a theme we refer to as the **"interstitial thread."** We believe that audiences can become overwhelmed by the burden of witnessing risky stories on such a heavy theme, and while the need for information is crucial, it can become too heavy of a creative meal to digest; for this reason, the "interstitials" become welcome, often light-hearted breaks to help ease the journey through this hour-long event.

Weaving together these three threads is an act of generosity, patience, and acknowledgment that many good ideas may have to be excised in order to ensure an audience-friendly, entertaining, and informative event. What emerges after fifteen weeks of arduous work is a play, approximately one hour in length, that engages the audience at an emotional, intellectual, and hopefully an activist experience. The performance is shared for a carefully invited crowd that includes advocates and skeptics of RJ alike in order to ensure a real dialog rather than a performance for like-minded individuals. After the hour-long event, the audience are invited to select scenes with which they would like to engage. These policy scenes are remounted theatrically and audience members, invited on-stage, move from being spectators to becoming "spect-actors" (Boal, 1992, p. 208).

The Performance Dialogs

The primary purpose of the PPJP experience is to restore dialog to a process that has too often been informed by political obfuscation and a monologic imposition of policy upon a people either uninformed or disempowered. This dialog occurs as the culmination of a fifteen-week experience where stories have been cultivated, harvested, and curated in the service of sociopolitical, cultural, or spiritual transformation around the issue of criminal justice. A play has been prepared and rehearsed, primarily by non-actors, for an audience who will become more than spectators, in the service of creating what Freire would deem a *problematizing* space—that is to say, a space that invites "a pedagogy or teaching methodology that creates the conditions for thinkingdoing" (Lawton, 2022, p. 55). The end result of this public artistic dialog is not the production of answers so much as the invitation to become more troubled by the status quo.

Audience members are recruited from within the families of enrolled students, the friends and family of our partners at HDA, and stakeholders in the criminal justice system. Far from perfect, the PPJP experience had nonetheless brought hundreds of students into close dialog with dozens of advocates of restorative justice with direct experience as survivors and former offenders of violence.

The combined creative work has produced five plays in five years which have been witnessed by hundreds of audience members for whom the experience has left a lasting impression.[4] Students enrolled in the course have shared that the course was "a really productive, life-changing experience," "it put me in someone's shoes," "it completely changed my perspective," and even "My friends who came ... were struck by how a piece that is devised [could] make social change." Partners from HDA reported that the experience "portrayed the reality of what life is really like for people who are in the system," and "the power of story is transcendent. It can actually lift people up."

Partner Javier Stauring of HDA noted that policymakers and other legislative representatives had attended the performances through the years, and this presence seemed to help shed light on the work that organizations like HDA were doing. Although it is not possible to prove, Stauring speculated that performance opportunities like PPJP helped humanize the issue of RJ and opened policymakers to the need for increased fiscal and legislative support of such programs.

Some thirty students from Price School of Public Policy and the School of Dramatic Arts are working on the sixth annual PPJP experience, scheduled for public performance and dialog in April, 2024. The engagement of theory and practice in this interactive arena represents the heart of what Paulo Freire and Augusto Boal may have imagined, but the limitations are also present. The play reaches only 100 spect-actors each year. The core team is already imaging the next steps needed to amplify this message, including ideas to bring scenes and workshops into detention facilities and within victims' groups.

As Boal would remind us, PPJP is not a revolution, but rather a "rehearsal for the revolution" (1979, p. 122).

Notes

1   Including the former stand-alone model of the Theatre in the Community class before its partnership with the Topics in Public Policy and Urban Studies course began in Spring, 2019.

2   A body of techniques from the canon of Theatre of the Oppressed employing embodied image-making to tell complex stories without words. This ensures a democratization of the story and it offers a buffer against concretizing a theme which may be better suited if left open to interpretation and more expansive, community-based ideas or input.

3   In the context of TO work, that is to say which scenes are open to audience interventions in Forum Theatre style—where the unfamiliar audience member may be invited to replace the protagonist and offer different solutions. In risky stories, this could be problematic at best, re-traumatizing at worst.

4   They are, in order: *On This Day* (2019); *Pause* (2020); *Waging Witness* (2021); *Mother—Monster—Survivor* (2022); and *Too Soon* (2023).

References

Anderson, J. (2019). America spends much more on prisoners than students — here's why. Go Banking Rates. May 27. https://www.gobankingrates.com/money/economy/states-that-spend-more-on-prisons-than-education/.

Applied theatre programs — a comprehensive list. Theatre Trip. (January 23, 2024). https://www.theatretrip.com/applied-theatre-programs/#GCanada.

Blair, B. (2024). *THTR 488: Theatre in the community, course syllabus*. Los Angeles, CA: University of Southern California.

Boal, A. (1979). *Theatre of the oppressed*. New York, NY: Theatre Communications Group.

Boal, A. (1992). *Games for actors and non-actors*. London: Routledge.

Freire, P. (1970/2000). *Pedagogy of the oppressed*. London: Continuum.

Freire, P. (1985). *The politics of education: Culture, power, and liberation*. London: Bergin & Garvey.

Freire, P., & Macedo, D. (1987). *Literacy: Reading the word & the world*. London: Taylor & Francis Group.

Homepage. Healing dialogue and action (February 18, 2021). Retrieved August 26, 2022, from https://www.ecoelite.org/.

Lawton, P. (2022). Paolo Freire's "Conscientization." *Research on Steiner Education*, 13(1), 49–65.

Salverson, J. (1997). Performing emergency: Witnessing, popular theatre, and the lie of the literal. *Theatre Topics*, 6(2), 181–91.

Sloane, D. (2024). *PPD 400: Topics in public policy and urban studies, course syllabus*. Los Angeles, CA: University of Southern California.

Zehr, H. (1990). *Changing lenses: A new focus for crime and justice*. Scottdale, PA; Waterloo: Herald Press.

Zehr, H., & Sawin, J. L. (2006). The ideas of engagement and empowerment. In G. Johnstone, & D. V. Ness (Eds.), *Handbook of restorative justice* (1st ed.) (pp. 183–4). London: Routledge.

INDEX